ALL-TIME-FAVORITE RECIPES *From* FLORIDA COOKS

Dedication

For every cook who wants to create amazing recipes from the great state of Florida.

Appreciation

Thanks to all our Florida cooks who shared their delightful and delicious recipes with us!

Gooseberry Patch
An imprint of Globe Pequot
246 Goose Lane
Guilford, CT 06437
www.gooseberrypatch.com
1 800 854 6673

978-162093-365-7

Printed in Korea.

Do you have a tried & true recipe...tip, craft or memory that you'd like to see featured in a *Gooseberry Patch* cookbook? Visit our website at www.gooseberrypatch.com and follow the easy steps to submit your favorite family recipe.

Or send them to us at:

Gooseberry Patch
PO Box 812
Columbus, OH 43216-0812

Don't forget to include the number of servings your recipe makes, plus your name, address, phone number and email address. If we select your recipe, your name will appear right along with it... and you'll receive a FREE copy of the book!

FLORIDA COOKS

THE SUNSHINE STATE

Why is Florida called the Sunshine State? Easy enough. It depends on where you are, of course, but bragging rights for sunny days are anywhere from 230 to 260 days per year. No wonder the state's climate is referred to as tropical or subtropical.

That all translates into citrus crops. Oranges are the leading cash crop. Other important citrus fruits include grapefruit, tangerines, limes and tangelos. Primary citrus groves are n central and southern parts of the state. Peanuts, also a arge crop, thrive in northern and western Florida. Farmers n southern parts work with other tropical and semitropical fruits, such as bananas, avocados, papayas, mangoes and pineapples. Throughout the state, watermelons, strawberries and cantaloupes thrive.

Florida is one of the leading states in sugar cane production, especially in the region of the Everglades. Other field crops nclude soybeans, cotton, corn, oats, hay, wheat and tobacco. And don't forget the fishing industry. Florida is one of the eading commercial fishing states. Leading catches are obsters and shrimp. Other important commercial fishes nclude grouper, catfish, mackerel, red snapper, blue and stone crabs, clams and shark.

The amazing cooks from the Sunshine State have shared recipes that are dear to their hearts. You'll find everything from Cinnamon-Banana Muffins and Chunky Tomato-Avocado Salad to Grilled Pineapple Sundaes and Key Lime Cupcakes. We know you will love this collection of tried & true recipes from cooks from all around the great state of Florida. Enjoy!

OUR STORY

Back in 1984, our families were neighbors in little Delaware, Ohio. With small children, we wanted to do what we loved and stay home with the kids too. We had always shared a love of home cooking and so, **Gooseberry Patch** was born.

Almost immediately, we found a connection with our customers and it wasn't long before these friends started sharing recipes. Since then we've enjoyed publishing hundreds of cookbooks with your tried & true recipes.

We know we couldn't have done it without our friends all across the country and we look forward to continuing to build a community with you. Welcome to the **Gooseberry Patch** family!

JoAnn & Vickie

TABLE OF CONTENTS

CHAPTER ONE

Good-Start Breakfast & Brunch

THE SUNSHINE IS CALLING AND YOU WILL BE READY TO ENJOY EVERY MINUTE WHEN YOU SERVE THESE BRIGHTEN-YOUR-DAY DISHES FOR A GOOD-MORNING BREAKFAST OR BRUNCH.

CINNAMON-BANANA MUFFINS

JULIE DOSSANTOS
FORT PIERCE, FL

This is a basic banana bread recipe, and who doesn't like banana bread? These muffins have a few added ingredients for extra flavor!

1/2 c. butter, softened
1 c. sugar
2 eggs, beaten
1/4 c. applesauce
1 T. cinnamon
1 T. vanilla extract
2 c. all-purpose flour
1 t. baking soda
3 ripe bananas, mashed

1 In a bowl, beat butter and sugar with an electric mixer on low speed until blended. Beat in eggs, applesauce, cinnamon and vanilla; set aside.

2 In a separate large bowl, mix together flour and baking soda; add butter mixture and stir until blended. Add bananas; mix thoroughly. Pour batter into paper-lined muffin tins, filling 2/3 full.

3 Bake at 350 degrees for 25 minutes. May also pour batter into a greased 9"x5" loaf pan; bake for one hour.

Makes 1-1/2 to 2 dozen muffins or one loaf

FLORIDA FUN

A "must-have" picker-upper, of course, is fresh orange juice. Go to a fancy-schmancy juice bar, if you must, or squeeze it yourself at home. YUM.

ANGIE'S EASY PANCAKES

EVANGELINE BOSTON
BRADENTON, FL

I have been using this recipe for more than 30 years and my kids grew up on them. It's easy, no-fail and tastes so good, even plain. There's no need to buy pancake mix...you have it all in your pantry!

2 c. all-purpose flour
1/2 c. sugar
4-1/2 t. baking powder
1 t. salt
2 eggs, beaten
2 c. milk
1/4 c. butter, melted and slightly cooled
Optional:
1/2 c. blueberries, chocolate chips or chopped pecans
Garnish: butter, pancake syrup

1 In a large bowl, combine flour, sugar, baking powder and salt; mix well and set aside.

2 In a separate bowl, whisk together eggs, milk and melted butter. Add egg mixture to flour mixture; stir until all big lumps are gone. Stir in optional ingredients, if desired.

3 Spoon batter onto a greased hot griddle by 1/4 cupfuls. Cook until golden on both sides. Serve topped with butter and syrup. Leftover pancakes freeze well.

Makes 12 to 15, 5-inch pancakes

COUNTRY WHEAT CRACKERS

JOANN
GOOSEBERRY PATCH

These crisp, hearty homemade crackers are a real treat. We love to have them with fried eggs!

1 c. whole-wheat flour
1 c. all-purpose flour
1/2 t. baking powder
1/2 t. salt
2 T. butter, diced
1/3 c. water
1 T. whipping cream
Garnish: butter

1 Mix flours, baking powder and salt in a bowl. Cut in butter with 2 knives until mixture resembles coarse meal. Add water and cream; stir to form a stiff dough.

2 Pat the dough out thinly on an ungreased 15"x10" jelly-roll pan. Score into 16 squares; pierce each square several times with a fork. Bake at 300 degrees for 45 minutes. Cool on pan; break apart and store in an airtight container. Serve with butter.

Makes 16

WEEKEND PANCAKES

SOPHIA GRAVES
OKEECHOBEE, FL

At least one day during the weekend we have pancakes in my house. When my niece and nephews visit, they always request these for breakfast.

1-1/4 c. all-purpose flour
1 T. baking powder
1 T. sugar
1 T. butter, melted and cooled slightly
1 egg, beaten
1 t. vanilla extract
1 to 1-1/4 c. milk, divided

1 Mix together flour, baking powder and sugar in a large bowl. In a separate bowl, stir together butter, egg, vanilla and one cup milk. Pour butter mixture over flour mixture; mix well. If batter is too thick, add additional milk to desired consistency.

2 Pour batter by 1/4 cupfuls onto a hot, lightly greased griddle. Cook until batter starts to bubble, about 3 minutes. Flip pancakes and cook an additional 2 to 3 minutes.

Serves 8

AUTUMN EGG BAKE

JULIE DOSSANTOS
FORT PIERCE, FL

We love eating breakfast for dinner. This is a great dish to prepare ahead of time and pop in the oven any time of day! Serve with warm pumpkin muffins for a yummy autumn meal.

6 eggs
4 egg whites
1-1/2 t. nutmeg
6 slices turkey bacon, crisply cooked and crumbled
1 c. fresh baby spinach
1/2 c. shredded Parmesan cheese
1/4 c. onion, diced
salt and pepper to taste

1 In a bowl, beat together eggs, egg whites and nutmeg. Pour into an 11"x9" baking pan sprayed with non-stick vegetable spray. Add remaining ingredients; stir gently.

2 Bake, uncovered, at 350 degrees for 20 to 25 minutes, until eggs are cooked through.

Serves 4 to 6

GG'S PANCAKE SAUSAGE BREAKFAST

JULIE DOSSANTOS
FORT PIERCE, FL

This recipe is directly from my Grandma "GG." It brings back many wonderful childhood memories of family Christmases spent at my grandparents' home in Arkansas.

10 to 12 brown & serve breakfast sausages
2 c. pancake mix
1 c. milk
3 eggs, beaten
Garnish: maple syrup

1 Brown sausages according to package directions; drain on a paper towel-lined plate. In a bowl, combine pancake mix, milk and eggs. Blend well. Pour batter into a greased 13"x9" baking pan.

2 Arrange sausages in rows across the batter. Sausages will sink to the bottom. Bake at 350 degrees for 30 minutes, or until a toothpick tests clean. Cut into servings, allowing one sausage per serving. Serve with syrup.

Makes 10 to 12 servings

BLACK BEAN BREAKFAST BOWLS

VICKIE
GOOSEBERRY PATCH

I love black beans, so finding a tasty way to have them for breakfast makes me happy. Sometimes I sprinkle a bit of chopped, fresh cilantro on top for extra flavor.

2 T. olive oil
4 eggs, beaten
15-1/2 oz. can black beans, drained and rinsed
1 avocado, peeled, pitted and sliced
1/4 c. shredded Cheddar cheese
1/4 c. favorite salsa
salt and pepper to taste

1 Heat oil in a skillet over medium heat. Add eggs and scramble as desired, 3 to 5 minutes; remove from heat. Place beans in a microwave-safe bowl. Microwave on high until warm, one to 2 minutes.

2 To serve, divide beans among 4 bowls; top each bowl with eggs, avocado, cheese and salsa. Season with salt and pepper.

Makes 2 servings

BONUS IDEA

Fresh berries all year 'round, it's easy! Just line a cookie sheet with wax paper, spread berries in a single layer and freeze until solid. Remove from tray and place in a plastic freezer bag.

GRANDMA'S SPECIAL CORNBREAD BAKE

MARTHA STAPLER
SANFORD, FL

While making my usual cornbread, I decided to use up some items in the fridge. The result was really delicious!

- **2 bunches broccoli, cut into bite-size flowerets**
- **2 8-1/2 oz. pkgs. corn muffin mix**
- **2 onions, chopped**
- **1 small jalapeño pepper, seeded and minced**
- **salt and pepper to taste**
- **6 eggs, beaten**
- **1-1/2 c. milk**
- **8-oz. pkg. shredded sharp Cheddar cheese**

1 Bring a large saucepan of water to a boil over high heat. Add broccoli; cook for 3 to 4 minutes, until crisp-tender. Drain; transfer broccoli to a large bowl. Add dry corn muffin mix, onions and jalapeño pepper; season with salt and pepper. In a separate bowl, whisk together eggs and milk. Add to broccoli mixture; stir well.

2 Pour batter into a greased deep 11"x9" baking pan. Bake, uncovered, at 350 degrees for 40 minutes. Top with cheese; bake an additional 5 minutes, or until cheese is melted. Let stand for 20 minutes before slicing.

Makes 10 to 12 servings

ON-THE-GO BREAKFAST PARFAIT

KIM WILSON
MELBOURNE, FL

This parfait can be prepared the day before and then it's ready in the morning when you need it. If you're making it a day ahead, toss the apple with a little lemon juice to prevent darkening.

1/4 c. fresh or frozen raspberries
1/3 c. chopped walnuts
1 apple, peeled, cored and diced
1/2 c. vanilla yogurt
1/3 c. granola cereal

1 In a container with a lid, layer ingredients in the order given. Cover and refrigerate until ready to eat. Stir up ingredients just before serving.

Makes one serving

BANANA PANCAKE TOPPER

BETH KRAMER,
PORT SAINT LUCIE, FL

Perfect for a brunch! Top your favorite pancakes with a spoonful of these luscious bananas and warmed syrup.

2 bananas, sliced
2 T. butter, melted

1 In a large skillet over medium heat, cook bananas in butter for 2 to 3 minutes per side, until golden.

Serves 4 to 6

GRANNY'S BISCUITS

SANDRA CROOK
JACKSONVILLE, FL

I have used this recipe for many years. It's a true "Southern biscuit!" Just add sausage gravy for a wonderful down-home breakfast.

4 c. self-rising flour
3 t. sugar
3 t. baking powder
1-1/2 c. buttermilk
1/2 c. vegetable oil

1 In large bowl, mix self-rising flour, sugar, and baking powder. Make a well in the center. Pour in buttermilk and oil. Stir until blended. Shape dough and roll on a floured surface. Cut biscuits 1/2-inch thick. Place biscuits on an oiled baking sheet and bake at 400 degrees for 12 to 15 minutes.

Makes 24 biscuits

BROCCOLI QUICHE PEPPERS

CHERI MAXWELL
GULF BREEZE, FL

We love these colorful peppers for a brunch dish that's just a little different. Sprinkle with mozzarella cheese, if desired, after you take the peppers from the oven.

4 red, yellow or green peppers, tops cut off and reserved
1 c. broccoli, finely chopped
4 eggs
1/2 c. milk
1/2 t. garlic powder
1/4 t. Italian seasoning

1 Finely dice reserved tops of peppers; set aside. Place pepper shells upright in custard cups; set cups in a 9"x9" baking pan. Spoon 1/4 cup broccoli into each pepper; set aside. In a bowl, whisk together eggs, milk, diced peppers and seasonings; pour evenly into peppers.

2 Bake, uncovered, at 325 degrees for 40 to 50 minutes, until peppers are tender and egg mixture is set. Let stand 5 minutes before serving.

Makes 4 servings

HERBED MUSHROOM OMELETS

JO ANN
GOSEBERRY PATCH

I like to serve this omelet on weekends when we have plenty of time to enjoy it. Add some crumbled bacon if you like.

- **4 to 6 eggs, beaten**
- **1 T. fresh parsley, chopped**
- **1 t. fresh oregano, chopped**
- **1/2 t. fresh thyme, chopped**
- **salt and pepper to taste**
- **2 t. butter, divided**
- **1-1/2 c. sliced mushrooms**

1 Whisk together eggs and seasonings; set aside. Melt one teaspoon butter in a skillet over medium heat. Add mushrooms and sauté until tender; remove from skillet and set aside.

2 Melt 1/2 teaspoon butter in skillet over low heat; pour in half the egg mixture. Stir eggs around in skillet with a spatula to cook evenly. Lift edges to allow uncooked egg to flow underneath. When almost cooked, spoon on half the mushrooms and fold over. Repeat with remaining egg mixture.

Serves 2

MAPLE BREAKFAST BUNDLES

RACHEL KOWASIC
VALRICO, FL

A quick and delicious all-in-one breakfast!

- **12-oz. tube refrigerated biscuits**
- **2 to 4 T. pure maple syrup**
- **5 slices American cheese, halved**
- **5 brown & serve breakfast sausage patties, prepared and halved**

1 On a floured surface, roll out biscuits into 8 to 10-inch circles. Spread each biscuit with maple syrup; top with a half-slice of cheese and a half-slice of sausage.

2 Roll up into a bundle, folding in sides of biscuits over toppings. Place on an ungreased baking sheet; drizzle with additional syrup. Bake at 350 degrees for about 20 minutes, until golden.

Makes 10 servings

ROSEMARY-SEA SALT BREAD

MATT MCCURDY
SAINT PETERSBURG, FL

After my girlfriend moved out of state, I needed to learn how to cook and bake! Having zero cooking skills, I looked for recipes even I could do. Through trial & error I came up with this delicious bread.

4 c. bread flour
3 to 4 t. vital wheat gluten flour
2 t. active dry yeast
2 T. fresh rosemary, chopped and divided
2 t. sea salt, divided
2 t. extra-virgin olive oil, divided
2 c. warm water
2 t. cornmeal

1 In a large bowl, combine flours, yeast, one tablespoon rosemary, one teaspoon salt and one teaspoon olive oil. Heat water until very warm, about 110 to 115 degrees; add to flour mixture. Stir together until well blended; cover with plastic wrap. To allow flavor to develop, let stand at room temperature for about one hour, then refrigerate overnight up to 4 days.

2 Before baking, let bowl stand at room temperature for one hour. Turn out dough onto a lightly floured surface; give dough a stretch or two. Line a baking sheet with parchment paper; sprinkle with cornmeal.

3 Shape dough into a round loaf and place on baking sheet. Combine remaining salt, olive oil and rosemary in a small bowl; brush over dough. Spritz a little water into preheated oven.

4 Bake at 475 degrees for 30 minutes; reduce to 400 degrees and bake for 10 additional minutes. Remove loaf to a wire rack. Cool completely before slicing.

Makes one loaf, about 12 servings

SPINACH & TOMATO FRENCH TOAST

LINDA BONWILL
ENGLEWOOD, FL

A healthier way to make French toast...plus, it looks so pretty!

- 3 eggs
- salt and pepper to taste
- 8 slices Italian bread
- 4 c. fresh spinach, torn
- 2 tomatoes, sliced
- Garnish: grated Parmesan cheese

1 In a bowl, beat eggs with salt and pepper. Dip bread slices into egg. Place in a lightly greased skillet over medium heat; cook one side until lightly golden.

2 Place fresh spinach and 2 slices of tomato onto each slice, pressing lightly to secure. Flip and briefly cook on other side until golden.

Serves 4

WHOLE-WHEAT PUMPKIN BREAD

JULIE DOSSANTOS
FORT PIERCE, FL

Toasted pumpkin bread with cream cheese is our breakfast tradition for Halloween and Thanksgiving. Also wonderful for a late-night snack!

- 3-1/2 c. whole-wheat flour
- 3 c. sugar
- 2 t. baking soda
- 1-1/2 t. salt
- 2 t. cinnamon
- 2 t. nutmeg
- 1 c. oil
- 15-oz. can pumpkin
- 4 eggs, beaten
- 2/3 c. water
- 1-1/2 t. vanilla extract

1 Spray two 9"x5" loaf pans with non-stick vegetable spray; set aside. In a large bowl, combine flour, sugar, baking soda, salt and spices; mix well. Add oil, pumpkin, eggs, water and vanilla. Beat with an electric mixer on low speed until combined.

2 Pour half of batter into each loaf pan. Bake at 350 degrees for 55 minutes to an hour, until loaves test done with a toothpick inserted in the center. Cool loaves in pans on a wire rack for 15 minutes; turn out of pans.

Makes 2 loaves

SWEET BACON MONKEY BREAD

POLLY MCCALLUM
PALATKA, FL

A new take on monkey bread that everyone is sure to love!

6 slices bacon
2 T. butter
2 T. maple syrup
1/4 c. brown sugar, packed
1/4 t. cinnamon
2 8-oz. tubes refrigerated crescent dinner rolls

1 In a skillet over medium heat, cook bacon until crisp; drain on paper towels. Combine butter and syrup in a microwave-safe bowl. Microwave on high, uncovered, for 30 to 45 seconds, until hot. Add brown sugar and cinnamon; stir until dissolved.

2 Spray an 8"x4" loaf pan with non-stick vegetable spray; gently pour butter mixture into pan. Crumble bacon over top. Unroll one tube of rolls into a large rectangle; press perforations to seal. Cut rectangle into 8 rows by 3 rows, to make 24 pieces. Repeat with remaining tube.

3 Form each piece of dough into a ball; layer balls in pan. Bake at 350 degrees for 30 to 35 minutes, until golden. Cool in pan 5 minutes. Place a serving plate over pan; carefully turn out onto plate. Serve warm.

Serves 8

CHAPTER TWO

Sunshiny Salads & Sides

WITH FRESH PRODUCE ALWAYS NEARBY, IT IS A JOY TO MAKE FLORIDA-STYLE SALADS, AND SATISFYING SIDES THAT EASILY STAND ALONE AS A LIGHT LUNCH OR ACCOMPANY ANY MAIN DISH.

BAKED HAM MACARONI & CHEESE

JULIE HUTSON
CALLAHAN, FL

I simply love good old comfort food. This mac & cheese is very different from my traditional recipe, but it is spectacular! It has a creamy, cheesy texture with a little bit of spicy love from the pimento and cayenne pepper. It makes a ton of pasta, so be prepared to feed a crowd or freeze half for later.

16-oz. pkg. penne pasta or elbow macaroni, uncooked
1/4 c. butter
1/2 c. all-purpose flour
4 c. milk
2 8-oz. pkgs. cream cheese, softened
1/2 t. cayenne pepper
16-oz. pkg. shredded Cheddar cheese, divided
2 c. cooked ham, diced
4-oz. jar chopped pimentos, drained

1 Cook pasta or macaroni according to package directions; drain and set aside. Melt butter in a large saucepan over medium heat. Whisk in flour; cook until lightly golden. Pour in milk, whisking constantly. Continue to cook until thickened and creamy.

2 Add cream cheese, cayenne pepper and 3 cups Cheddar cheese to milk mixture; stir until cheeses are melted. Remove from heat. Combine cooked pasta, cheese mixture, ham and pimentos; transfer to a greased 3-quart casserole dish. Top with remaining Cheddar cheese.

3 Bake, uncovered, at 375 degrees for 45 to 50 minutes, until hot and bubbly.

Makes 8 to 10 servings

DIANE'S POTATO SALAD

CHRISTINE WHEELER
JUPITER, FL

A friend of mine uses this recipe when she caters. It is easy to make and so delicious...my family loves it!

5 lbs. redskin potatoes, cooked and cubed
8 to 12 eggs, hard-boiled, peeled and chopped
1 lb. bacon, crisply cooked and crumbled
1 to 2 bunches green onions, chopped
16-oz. jar mayonnaise
16-oz. jar mayonnaise-style salad dressing
salt and pepper to taste

1 In a large serving bowl, combine potatoes, eggs, bacon and onions; set aside. In a separate bowl, combine remaining ingredients.

2 Gently fold mayonnaise mixture into potato mixture. Cover and chill at least 2 hours before serving.

Makes 10 to 12 servings

FRESH FIESTA CORN SALAD

KRISTY WELLS
OCALA, FL

Living here in Florida, fresh corn is readily available most of the summer. This was made often for my family's get-togethers or for a quick snack with tortilla chips after church before lunch was ready.

4 ears sweet corn
10-oz. can diced tomatoes with green chiles
1/4 c. fresh cilantro, coarsely chopped
1/4 c. green onions, chopped
1/2 c. ranch salad dressing
2 T. lime juice
Optional: tortilla chips

1 Cut corn kernels off the cobs; place in a serving bowl. Add tomatoes with juice and remaining ingredients except tortilla chips. Mix gently until combined.

2 Serve as a salad, or with tortilla chips as a snack. May cover and refrigerate up to 3 days.

Serves 6 to 8

APPLE-CINNAMON COLESLAW

MARIE WARNER
JENNINGS, FL

I love simple coleslaw combos. Adding just a touch of fruit and spice turns coleslaw into a grand side dish.

2 c. cabbage, shredded
1-1/2 c. Granny Smith apples, cored and chopped
1/2 c. chopped walnuts, pecans or almonds
1/2 c. brown or golden raisins

1 Combine all ingredients in a bowl; toss to mix. Pour Dressing over top; toss again. Serve immediately, or cover and refrigerate.

Makes 4 to 6 servings

DRESSING
8-oz. container vanilla yogurt
1/2 t. cinnamon
1/4 c. frozen apple juice concentrate, thawed

1 In a small bowl, combine all ingredients; blend well.

KITCHEN TIP

Make extra salad dressing and keep in the refrigerator for a last-minute salad topper.

CHICKEN & RICE SALAD

FRANCIE STUTZMAN
NORTH FORT MYERS, FL

This dish is scrumptious...I hope you'll try it!

- 3 T. red wine vinegar
- 1-1/2 T. extra-virgin olive oil
- 1/4 t. pepper
- 1 clove garlic, minced
- 2 c. long-grain rice, cooked
- 1-1/2 c. cooked chicken breast, diced
- 1/2 c. jarred roasted red peppers, drained and diced
- 1/2 c. Kalamata olives, pitted and halved
- 1/4 c. fresh chives, chopped
- 1/4 c. fresh basil, chopped
- 1/4 c. fresh oregano, chopped
- 14-oz. can artichokes, drained and diced
- 4-oz. pkg. crumbled feta cheese

1 In a small bowl, whisk together vinegar, olive oil, pepper and garlic. Set aside. In a separate bowl, combine rice and remaining ingredients except cheese.

2 At serving time, drizzle vinegar mixture over salad; sprinkle with cheese.

Makes 4 servings

SCARLETT'S CORN PUDDING

SCARLETT HEDDEN
PORT SAINT JOHN, FL

This dish has been in my favorite recipes for quite awhile. It is low in calories, fat and cholesterol and it tastes delicious. Serve it to company and they won't even know they're eating healthy!

- **2 c. evaporated milk**
- **1-1/2 c. egg substitute**
- **2 T. butter, melted**
- **1/4 c. all-purpose flour**
- **1/4 c. stevia powdered sweetener**
- **2 t. baking powder**
- **1/2 t. salt substitute**
- **6 c. fresh corn kernels, or frozen corn, thawed and drained**

1 In a large bowl, combine milk, egg substitute and butter; set aside. In a small bowl, combine flour, stevia, baking powder and salt substitute; add to milk mixture and stir until smooth. Stir in corn.

2 Spoon into a 13"x9" baking pan coated with non-stick vegetable spray. Bake, uncovered, at 350 degrees for 40 to 45 minutes, until set and golden. Let stand 5 minutes before serving.

Makes 8 servings

GARDEN PATCH GRILLED VEGETABLES

JO ANN
GOOSEBERRY PATCH

So beautiful to look at and so yummy to eat. Just put out the toothpicks and watch the veggies disappear!

- **6 small onions, sliced into wedges**
- **5 thin carrots, peeled**
- **3 potatoes, sliced into wedges**
- **1 red pepper, sliced into strips**
- **1 green pepper, sliced into strips**
- **2 zucchini, sliced lengthwise**
- **1/4 lb. mushrooms**
- **3 T. olive oil**
- **1/4 c. fresh thyme, chopped**
- **1/4 t. salt**
- **1/4 t. pepper**
- **salt and pepper to taste**

1 Cover onions, carrots and potatoes with water in a large saucepan. Simmer mixture over medium-high heat until crisp-tender, about 15 to 20 minutes. Drain; cool slightly.

2 Combine cooked and uncooked vegetables in a large bowl. Whisk together oil and thyme; drizzle half of mixture over vegetables. Arrange vegetables on a lightly oiled grill pan over medium-high heat. Grill until tender, turning often and brushing with remaining oil mixture. Sprinkle with salt and pepper; serve warm.

Makes 10 servings

CRACKER-STUFFED SQUASH

DENISE JONES
FOUNTAIN, FL

My mother always made this yummy side dish and I loved it... it's the only way I would eat squash as a youngster. Now that I'm older and wiser, I'll eat delicious squash almost any way it's cooked...but Mother's way is still a favorite!

5 yellow squash, trimmed
1 T. butter
2 eggs, beaten
2 c. saltine cracker crumbs
garlic powder, salt and pepper to taste
2 T. water
Optional: 1/2 c. onion, chopped

1 Place whole squash in a large saucepan with just enough water to cover. Bring to a boil over medium-high heat. Reduce heat and simmer 7 minutes, until tender. Drain and cool.

2 Melt butter in a skillet over medium heat. Cut squash in half lengthwise and scoop out insides into skillet. Add remaining ingredients; cook and stir until golden. Stuff squash halves with cracker mixture; arrange in a lightly greased 3-quart casserole dish. Pour water into the bottom of the dish.

3 Bake, uncovered, at 325 degrees for 25 to 30 minutes, until golden.

Makes 10 servings

CHUNKY TOMATO-AVOCADO SALAD

ALMA EVANS
PATRICK AFB, FL

Let it sit for at least 2 hours if you don't have time to refrigerate overnight.

1 avocado, pitted, peeled and cubed
3 plum tomatoes, chopped
1/4 c. sweet onion, chopped
1 T. fresh cilantro, chopped
2 to 3 T. lemon juice

1 Gently stir ingredients together; cover and refrigerate overnight.

Makes 4 servings

OVEN-FRIED EGGPLANT

FRANCES CLICK
HERNANDO BEACH, FL

My family enjoys fried eggplant, but we've been making an effort to eat healthier. This recipe has less fat and tastes delicious. It's one of our favorites.

1 c. Italian-seasoned dry bread crumbs
1 egg
2 T. olive oil
1 eggplant, sliced 1/4-inch thick

1 Place bread crumbs in a shallow dish; whisk together egg and oil in another shallow dish. Dip eggplant slices into egg mixture; roll in bread crumbs. Place slices on an ungreased baking sheet.

2 Bake at 375 degrees until tender and golden, about 15 to 20 minutes. May be frozen and reheated.

Serves 4 to 6

EXTRA-CHEESY MAC & CHEESE

VALARIE DENNARD
PALATKA, FL

The first time I served this recipe, my husband said it was by far the best macaroni & cheese he had ever eaten. It's a classic comfort food during the colder months of fall.

8-oz. pkg. shredded Italian 3-cheese blend
8-oz. pkg. shredded sharp Cheddar cheese
2 eggs, lightly beaten
12-oz. can evaporated milk
1-1/2 c. milk
1 t. salt
3/4 t. dry mustard
1/4 t. cayenne pepper
1/2 t. pepper
2-1/2 c. small shell pasta, uncooked

1 In a bowl, combine cheeses; set aside. In a separate bowl, whisk together remaining ingredients except pasta. Add pasta and 3 cups cheese mixture; stir well.

2 Spoon pasta mixture into a lightly greased slow cooker. Sprinkle with 3/4 cup cheese mixture; refrigerate remaining mixture. Cover slow cooker and cook on low setting for 4 hours, until cheese is melted and creamy and pasta is tender. Sprinkle servings evenly with remaining cheese mixture.

Serves 6 to 8

END-OF-THE-GARDEN RELISH

CHERI MAXWELL
GULF BREEZE, FL

When I was growing up, I always got to spend the last couple weeks of my summer vacation at my grandparents' home in the country. Grandma was justifiably proud of her big backyard garden. She would send me out with a basket to find the last of the vegetables growing there, so she could make this relish that we all loved. Just a taste of it still brings back such memories!

- **8 c. green tomatoes, cored and chopped**
- **4 c. red tomatoes, cored, peeled and chopped**
- **4 c. cabbage, chopped**
- **3 c. onions, chopped**
- **2 c. celery, chopped**
- **1 c. green peppers, chopped**
- **1 c. red peppers, chopped**
- **1 c. cucumbers, chopped**
- **1/2 c. canning salt**
- **2 32-oz. bottles white vinegar**
- **4 c. brown sugar, packed**
- **2 cloves garlic, minced**
- **1 T. celery seed**
- **1 T. mustard seed**
- **1 T. cinnamon**
- **1 t. ground ginger**
- **1/2 t. ground cloves**
- **8 1-pint canning jars and lids, sterilized**

1 In a very large enameled stockpot, combine chopped vegetables and salt; toss to thoroughly. Cover and refrigerate for 12 to 18 hours. Transfer vegetables to a colander; drain thoroughly.

2 In the same stockpot, combine remaining ingredients. Simmer over medium-high heat for 10 minutes, stirring occasionally. Add vegetables; reduce heat and simmer, uncovered, for 30 minutes, stirring occasionally. Increase heat; bring to a boil.

3 Spoon vegetables and liquid into hot sterilized jars, leaving 1/2-inch headspace. Wipe rims; secure with lids and rings. Process in a boiling-water bath for 15 minutes. Set jars on a towel to cool. Check for seals.

Makes 8 jars

CREAMY POTATO MASHIES

JULIE DOSSANTOS
FORT PIERCE, FL

This is our go-to holiday side dish. It also makes great comfort food any day of the year! My daughter named the recipe...she is their biggest fan.

- **5 lbs. Yukon Gold potatoes, cut into quarters or chunks**
- **1/2 c. butter, room temperature**
- **1/2 c. whole milk or heavy cream**
- **3/4 c. sour cream**
- **8-oz. pkg. cream cheese, softened**
- **salt and pepper to taste**

1 Cover potatoes with water in a stockpot. Bring to a boil over medium-high heat. Reduce heat to medium and cook for 15 to 20 minutes, until fork-tender; do not overcook. Drain potatoes.

2 Transfer to a large bowl; add butter and milk or cream. Beat with an electric mixer on medium speed to desired consistency. Stir in sour cream, cream cheese and seasonings.

Makes 10 to 12 servings

GIRL SCOUT APPLES

JACKIE GARVIN
VALRICO, FL

Baked apples have always been "Girl Scout apples" to me, because I learned to make them in Girl Scouts, just like I did Toad-in-the-Hole. Out of all the activities we did in Girl Scouts, the cooking memories have stayed with me the most.

- **1/2 c. brown sugar, packed**
- **1/2 c. butter, softened**
- **1 t. cinnamon**
- **1/2 t. vanilla extract**
- **Optional: 2 to 3 drops lemon extract**
- **1-1/2 oz. pkg. raisins**
- **4 Granny Smith apples, cored with stem ends reserved**

1 In a bowl, combine all ingredients except apples. Stuff each apple with 1/4 of the brown sugar mixture. Plug the stem end back in. Place apples upright in a slow cooker.

2 Cover and cook on high setting for 3 to 4 hours, until apples are tender but not falling apart.

Makes 4 servings

MANDARIN ORANGE SALAD WITH RASPBERRY VINAIGRETTE

LIZ PLOTNICK-SNAY
GOOSEBERRY PATCH

Quick and easy to prepare, this salad is best topped with a sweet dressing like Raspberry Vinaigrette.

- **4 c. green or red leaf lettuce, torn into bite-size pieces**
- **3 mandarin oranges, peeled and sectioned**
- **1/2 c. walnut pieces, toasted**
- **1/2 red onion, sliced**

1 Combine all ingredients. Toss with 1/4 cup Raspberry Vinaigrette dressing.

Makes 4 servings

RASPBERRY VINAIGRETTE

- **1/2 c. raspberry vinegar**
- **1/4 c. seedless raspberry jam**
- **1 t. coriander or ground cumin**
- **1/4 t. salt**
- **1/4 t. pepper**
- **1/2 c. extra-virgin olive oil**

1 Combine first 5 ingredients in blender. Turn blender on high; gradually add oil. Chill.

Makes 1-1/4 cups

SWEET & SUNNY KALE SALAD

CARLA SLAJCHERT
TAMPA, FL

This is a recipe I came up with when we wanted a fresh side and didn't have much in the refrigerator. The dressing tenderizes the kale as it stands.

1 bunch fresh kale, stems removed
1 Gala apple, peeled, cored and diced
1/2 c. red onion, finely diced
1/4 c. sunflower seed kernels
1-oz. cube Parmesan cheese

1 Slice kale into thin ribbons. In a serving bowl, toss kale with apple, onion and sunflower seeds.

2 Using a vegetable peeler, shave slices of Parmesan over mixture. Drizzle with Dressing; let stand for 15 to 20 minutes before serving.

Makes 4 servings

DRESSING
2 t. cider vinegar
1 t. Dijon mustard
1 t. honey
3 T. extra-virgin olive oil
salt and pepper to taste

1 In a small bowl, combine vinegar, mustard and honey. Whisk in olive oil until combined. Season lightly with salt and pepper.

TURKEY FRUIT SALAD

BEVERLY MOCK
PENSACOLA, FL

Host a summertime luncheon with girlfriends, then serve this delicious salad.

3 c. cooked turkey, cubed
3/4 c. celery, chopped
1 c. seedless red grapes, halved
1/3 c. fresh pineapple, cubed
11-oz. can mandarin oranges, drained
1/4 c. chopped pecans
1/4 c. light mayonnaise-type salad dressing
1/8 t. salt
Garnish: lettuce leaves

1 Combine turkey, celery, grapes, pineapple, oranges and pecans together. Blend in salad dressing; sprinkle with salt.

2 Chill until serving time. When ready to serve, spoon individual servings onto lettuce leaves.

Serves 4

FLORIDA FUN

Allow yourself to be surprised. There are fancy, pricey restaurants, of course, but some of the tastiest finds might be in a gas station food stop. Seriously. Florida has great food everywhere!

HONEY-KISSED CARROTS

ELLEN FOLKMAN
CRYSTAL BEACH, FL

This is a favorite recipe in my home. I often cook the carrots in a steamer, then transfer to a bowl and add the remaining ingredients. It's easy to double for a larger crowd.

1 lb. carrots, peeled and sliced 1/2-inch thick
1/4 c. water
1/3 c. golden raisins
1/3 c. honey
2 T. butter

1 In a saucepan over medium heat, combine carrots and water. Cover and simmer 15 minutes, or until tender. Add remaining ingredients.

2 Simmer, uncovered, until carrots are glazed, about 10 minutes, stirring occasionally.

Makes 4 servings

PRESENTATION

When serving a salad with cheese, herbs or spices, set out additional small bowls of each so more can be added if desired.

MOMMA'S CUKES & SOUR CREAM

NANCY ERNEY
MCINTOSH, FL

One of Mom's recipes that she could start and then leave for me to finish while she was at work.

2 regular cucumbers or 4 Kirby cucumbers, peeled and sliced
1 sweet onion, sliced
1/2 c. sour cream
2 T. white vinegar
1 T. plus 1 t. mayonnaise
1 t. seasoned salt
1/4 t. salt
1/8 t. pepper
Optional: chopped fresh or dried parsley

1 Combine cucumbers and onion in a large bowl. Place several paper towels on top; chill in refrigerator for at least one hour. In a small bowl, whisk together remaining ingredients except parsley.

2 Transfer cucumber mixture to a colander; drain excess liquid and pat dry with paper towels. Return cucumber mixture to bowl; pour on sour cream mixture and toss to mix. Garnish with parsley, if desired. Serve immediately, or cover and chill until serving time.

Makes 4 to 6 servings

NANNY'S HOT CHICKEN SALAD

JULIE HUTSON
CALLAHAN, FL

My grandmother was the epitome of a southern hostess. Every person who ever walked through her door was offered a slice of pound cake or a homemade cookie. And she loved a party! Whenever someone mentioned they were planning a get-together, she would ask what she could bring. This is one of my all-time favorite recipes from her library.

3 boneless, skinless chicken breasts, cooked and cubed
2 c. cooked rice
2 c. shredded sharp Cheddar cheese
1 c. celery, chopped
1 c. mayonnaise
1/4 c. sour cream
1 T. lemon juice
1/2 t. salt
1/2 t. pepper
1/2 sleeve round buttery crackers, crushed
2 T. butter, melted

1 In a large bowl, mix together all ingredients except crackers and butter. Spoon into a 3-quart casserole dish coated with non-stick vegetable spray. Sprinkle crackers over top; drizzle melted butter over crackers.

2 Bake at 350 degrees for 30 minutes, until bubbly and golden on top.

Makes 8 to 10 servings

SHRIMP TOSSED SALAD

AMY BLEICH
JACKSONVILLE, FL

A simply scrumptious mix that's super for hot summer days!

- **1 head lettuce, torn**
- **9-oz. pkg. baby spinach**
- **3 c. coleslaw mix**
- **8-oz. can sliced water chestnuts, drained**
- **1/4 to 1/2 c. golden raisins**
- **1/4 to 1/2 c. sweetened dried cranberries**
- **1/2 red pepper, very thinly sliced**
- **2-lb. pkg. frozen cooked shrimp, thawed**
- **1 carrot, peeled**
- **1/2 c. chow mein noodles**
- **Optional: chopped fresh dill**
- **Garnish: sweet-and-sour salad dressing**

1 In a large serving bowl, arrange half each of lettuce, spinach and coleslaw mix. Top with half each of water chestnuts, raisins and cranberries. Layer with remaining lettuce, spinach and coleslaw mix. Arrange red peppers around the edge of the salad. Arrange shrimp inside the pepper ring.

2 Using a vegetable peeler, make carrot curls; arrange in center of bowl. Sprinkle with remaining water chestnuts, raisins and cranberries. Just before serving, top with chow mein noodles. If desired, sprinkle dill over the shrimp. Serve with salad dressing.

Serves 6

ROASTED TOMATO-FETA BROCCOLI

LYUBA BROOKE
JACKSONVILLE, FL

This is such a simple and fast side. Don't let the easiness of it fool you...this dish is full of flavor and it's really healthy.

2 T. olive oil
2 c. broccoli flowerets
1 c. cherry tomatoes
1 t. lemon juice
dried parsley, salt and pepper to taste
1/2 c. crumbled feta cheese
Optional: additional olive oil

1 Heat oil in a skillet over medium heat. Add broccoli, tomatoes, lemon juice and seasonings; cook until vegetables are crisp-tender.

2 Transfer warm vegetable mixture to a large bowl and mix in cheese. Drizzle with additional olive oil, if desired.

Serves 2 to 4

TWICE-BAKED SWEET POTATOES

TIFFINI LYONS
NAPLES, FL

A delicious variation on the traditional sweet potato casserole.

6 sweet potatoes
1/2 c. plus 1 T. butter, melted and divided
6 T. apple juice
2 T. brown sugar, packed
1/2 t. ground ginger
1 c. mini marshmallows
1/3 c. sweetened flaked coconut

1 Bake sweet potatoes at 375 degrees for 50 to 60 minutes, until tender. Cool slightly. Partially slice potatoes lengthwise; scoop out centers, leaving 1/8-inch thick shells. Mash potato pulp in a medium bowl. Add 1/2 cup butter, apple juice, brown sugar and ginger; beat until fluffy. Spoon into shells.

2 Mix together marshmallows, coconut and remaining butter; spoon over potatoes. Bake at 350 degrees for 20 to 25 minutes, until heated through.

Makes 6 servings

SUMMER STRAWBERRY SALAD

KRISTY WELLS
OCALA, FL

Living in Florida, we are blessed to have fresh local strawberries from January and well into summer, so I try to use them as much as possible. This salad is so delicious and my picky little eaters love it, not to mention it's incredibly easy. Serve as a side or with a bowl of soup and fresh bread to make a meal of it. Hope y'all enjoy it!

- 2 6-oz. pkgs. baby greens or spring mix
- 6 to 8 strawberries, hulled and sliced
- 1/2 c. red onion, thinly sliced
- 1/2 c. candied pecans or walnuts
- 1/4 c. crumbled blue cheese
- 1/4 to 1/2 c. balsamic salad dressing

1 Combine all ingredients in a very large bowl. Toss to mix; serve immediately.

Makes 6 to 8 servings

FLORIDA FUN

The Florida Strawberry Festival in late February and early March is Plant City, is the winter strawberry capital of the world. The multi-day party draws huge crowds. Yes, strawberry shortcake might just be on the menu.

CHAPTER THREE

Satisfying

Soups & Sandwiches

YOU CAN SERVE SOUL-SOOTHING BOWLS OF GOODNESS AND STACKED-WITH-FRESHNESS SANDWICHES FLORIDA-STYLE WHEN YOU MAKE THEM USING THESE NO-FUSS RECIPES.

CHICKEN, WILD RICE & MUSHROOM SOUP

LYUBA BROOKE
JACKSONVILLE, FL

A new twist on an old recipe I had for chicken rice soup. The wild rice gives it such a nice flavor! The recipe may seem lengthy at first glance, but it's mostly simmering time...perfect for a cozy weekend.

4 chicken breasts
9 c. water
3 cloves garlic, minced
3 T. butter
2 shallots, sliced
1-1/2 c. baby portabella mushrooms, sliced
8-oz. pkg. wild rice, uncooked
1/2 c. heavy cream or milk
salt and pepper to taste

1 Combine chicken and water in a large saucepan. Bring to a boil over medium-high heat; reduce heat to low. Cover and simmer for 60 to 90 minutes.

2 Remove chicken to a bowl, reserving broth. Let chicken cool. Meanwhile, in a large stockpot over medium heat, sauté garlic in butter until fragrant. Add shallots and mushrooms; cook until almost tender. Add rice; cook and stir for 2 to 3 minutes. Add 7 cups reserved broth. Bring to a boil; reduce heat to medium-low.

3 Cover and cook, stirring occasionally, for 20 minutes. Dice chicken, discarding skin and bones; add chicken to soup. Cover and simmer for 15 to 20 minutes, until most of broth is absorbed. If more liquid is needed, add remaining broth, one cup at a time, to desired consistency. Stir in cream or milk; bring to a boil. Reduce heat to medium-low and simmer for another 15 to 20 minutes.

Makes 8 servings

DAD'S FAMOUS MINESTRONE

GLENN STRACQUALURSI
LAKELAND, FL

My dad made this tasty soup for years at his park's fundraiser events and never had any left by the end...this one's in honor of my dad.

- 4 carrots, peeled and sliced
- 1 c. celery, chopped
- 1 c. onion, chopped
- 5 to 6 red potatoes, diced
- 3 zucchini, sliced
- 14-1/2 oz. can diced tomatoes
- 15-oz. can cut green beans
- 8 cloves garlic, chopped
- 3 T. olive oil
- 1-1/2 t. dried basil
- 1 t. dried rosemary
- 2 T. dried parsley
- 1/2 t. sea salt
- 1/2 t. pepper
- 3 14-oz. cans chicken broth
- 12-oz. bottle cocktail vegetable juice
- 1 bunch escarole, chopped
- 15-oz. can garbanzo beans
- 15-oz. can cannellini beans
- 8-oz. pkg. ditalini pasta, uncooked
- Garnish: grated Parmesan cheese

1 To a slow cooker, add all ingredients in order listed except beans, pasta and garnish. Cover and cook on low setting for 8 hours.

2 After 8 hours, stir in beans and pasta; cook for one more hour. Top servings with cheese.

Serves 8 to 10

CROCKERY BLACK BEAN SOUP

BETH KRAMER
PORT SAINT LUCIE, FL

Rich and creamy, this thick soup is a meal in itself!

- **1 T. olive oil**
- **2 red onions, chopped**
- **1 red pepper, chopped**
- **1 green pepper, chopped**
- **4 cloves garlic, minced**
- **4 t. ground cumin**
- **12-oz. pkg. dried black beans, uncooked**
- **1 T. chopped green chiles**
- **7 c. hot water**
- **2 T. lime juice**
- **1 t. kosher salt**
- **1/4 t. pepper**
- **1 c. plain yogurt**
- **1/2 c. plum tomatoes, seeded and chopped**
- **Garnish: chopped fresh cilantro, lime wedges, halved plum tomatoes**

1 Heat oil in a skillet over medium-high heat. Add onions and peppers; sauté until tender. Stir in garlic and cumin; cook one minute.

2 Use a slotted spoon to transfer mixture to a slow cooker. Add beans, chiles and hot water. Cover and cook on high setting for 6 hours.

3 Transfer 2 cups bean mixture to a blender; purée until smooth. Return mixture to slow cooker; stir in remaining ingredients except garnish. Garnish servings as desired.

Makes 8 servings

DOWN-HOME CHICKEN NOODLE SOUP

SARAH ROY
TYNDALL AFB, FL

A tried & true recipe with lots of flavor...perfect for chilly nights cozied-up next to a bonfire or served to a loved one with the sniffles.

- **4 14-1/2 oz. cans chicken broth**
- **16-oz. pkg. baby carrots, chopped**
- **4 stalks celery, cut into 1/2-inch pieces**
- **1 T. fresh parsley, minced**
- **1/2 t. pepper**
- **1/2 t. cayenne pepper**
- **2-1/2 lbs. boneless, skinless chicken breasts**
- **3/4 c. onion, finely chopped**
- **1-1/2 t. mustard seed**
- **2 cloves garlic, halved**
- **8-oz. pkg. egg noodles, cooked**

1 Combine broth, carrots, celery, parsley and peppers in a slow cooker. Place chicken in broth mixture; set aside.

2 Combine onion, mustard seed and garlic in a thick square of cheesecloth; tie into a bundle. Add spice bundle to slow cooker. Cover and cook on low setting for 5 to 6 hours.

3 Remove chicken from slow cooker; shred and return to slow cooker. Discard spice bundle. Stir cooked noodles into soup; cover and cook for 15 minutes, or until warmed through.

Serves 6 to 8

ISABELA'S SPECIAL VEGGIE SOUP

JULIE DOSSANTOS
FORT PIERCE, FL

I created this recipe for my daughter Isabela when she had the flu. I wanted to give her yummy warm soup, full of fresh veggies and lots of feel-better goodness. Serve with crackers or crusty bread.

2 14-oz. cans chicken broth
14-oz. can low-sodium chicken broth
8 redskin potatoes, peeled and chopped
3 carrots, peeled and chopped
1/2 sweet onion, chopped
salt and pepper to taste
2 T. dill weed, divided
15-1/2 oz. can diced tomatoes
2 zucchini, chopped
2 yellow squash, chopped
1/2 lb. green beans, trimmed and cut into 1-inch pieces
9-oz. pkg. frozen peas
1/2 bunch green onions, chopped

1 In a large slow cooker, combine broths, potatoes, carrots, sweet onion, salt, pepper and one tablespoon dill weed. Cover and cook on high setting for one hour. Stir in remaining dill weed, tomatoes with juice and remaining ingredients except green onions.

2 Reduce setting to low; cover and cook for 4 to 6 hours. Stir in green onions in the last 30 minutes

Serves 6 to 8

LENTIL & HAM SOUP

EDYTHE BOUQUIO
HUDSON, FL

My mom used to make this soup on the stove, but it was a little too thin for me. So I converted it to a slow-cooker recipe, thickened it up and added some more spices for flavor. When she and her husband asked me for the recipe, I knew it was good! Serve with thick, buttery slices of crusty bread for a complete meal.

2 c. dried lentils
6 c. water
1 onion, chopped
2 stalks celery, chopped
2 carrots, peeled and chopped
salt and pepper to taste
1 meaty ham bone
2 to 3 T. all-purpose flour
1/3 c. water
3 T. browning and seasoning sauce

1 Combine all ingredients except flour, water and browning sauce in a slow cooker. Cover and cook on low setting for 4 to 6 hours, until lentils are soft. Remove ham from bone and stir back into soup, discarding bone.

2 In a bowl, combine flour, water and seasoning sauce; mix well. Drizzle flour mixture into soup; mix well. Cover and cook on high setting for an additional 30 minutes, or until thickened.

Serves 6 to 8

MEGAN'S CRAZY SPICY CHILI

MEGAN SABO
DAYTONA BEACH, FL

Mom gave me this easy chili recipe when I was learning to cook. After I'd made it for awhile, I decided to add a couple of things and now I have a spicy new version that's my very own.

1 lb. ground beef
1 onion, chopped
1/2 lb. spicy ground pork sausage
1/2 lb. andouille pork link sausage, sliced
2 15-1/2 oz. cans red kidney beans
2 14-1/2 oz. cans diced tomatoes
2 8-oz. cans tomato sauce
1 c. frozen corn
1-1/2 c. water
1-1/4 oz. pkg. chili seasoning mix
Garnish: sour cream, shredded Cheddar cheese, corn chips

1 In a large soup pot over medium-high heat, brown beef and onion; drain and set aside in a bowl. In the same pot, brown spicy sausage and andouille together; drain. Add beef mixture, undrained beans, undrained tomatoes and remaining ingredients except garnish.

2 Reduce heat to low and simmer for about one hour, stirring occasionally. Serve in individual bowls topped with sour cream, cheese and corn chips.

Serves 6 to 8

SCOTT JUNIOR'S FAVORITE STEW

JAMIE SEIFERT
WINDERMERE, FL

This is my own recipe that I would serve my son's high school basketball team whenever some of them came home with him before a game. The stew would vanish before they left for the game!

- 3-lb. beef chuck roast
- 1-1/2 oz. pkg. stew seasoning mix
- 2 15-oz. cans kidney beans
- 2 14-1/2 oz. cans lima beans
- 15-1/4 oz. can corn
- 14-1/2 oz. can green beans
- 14-1/2 oz. can Italian-style stewed tomatoes
- 6 potatoes, peeled and cubed
- 1/2 onion, chopped
- 1 c. baby carrots
- 1 T. chili powder
- 3/8 t. chipotle hot pepper sauce
- 3 cubes beef bouillon
- 2 c. water
- salt and pepper to taste

1 Combine beef, seasoning mix, undrained vegetables and remaining ingredients in a slow cooker.

2 Cover and cook on low setting for 6 to 8 hours, until roast is very tender. Using 2 forks, shred roast in slow cooker; stir into stew.

Serves 6 to 8

KITCHEN TIP

Use white pepper instead of black in cream-based and light-colored soups. You'll get all the flavor with no visible pepper specks.

SPICY CHICKEN-PUMPKIN SOUP

KIM WILSON
MELBOURNE, FL

In the fall, I stock up on cans of pumpkin and try to create as many recipes as I can with them. This one is definitely a keeper in our home...super-yummo!

1 T. oil
6 boneless, skinless chicken breasts, cut into 1-inch cubes
1 sweet onion, halved and thinly sliced
3 cloves garlic, minced
1 T. fresh ginger, peeled and minced
1/2 t. to 3/4 t. red pepper flakes
2 stalks celery, diced
2 carrots, peeled and diced
15-oz. can pumpkin
11.3-oz. can mango nectar
1/2 c. lime juice
1/2 c. creamy peanut butter
4 c. chicken broth
2 c. water
1/2 c. whipping cream
1 T. cornstarch
3 c. cooked jasmine rice
Garnish: minced fresh cilantro, minced green onion, chopped unsalted peanuts

1 Heat oil in a skillet over medium heat. Add chicken to oil; cook, stirring occasionally, for 3 minutes. Add onion, garlic, ginger and red pepper flakes to chicken mixture; cook for one to 2 minutes.

2 Spoon chicken mixture into a slow cooker. Add celery, carrots, pumpkin, nectar, lime juice, peanut butter, broth and water to chicken mixture; stir gently. Cover and cook on low setting for 8 hours. Mix together cream and cornstarch in a bowl; stir into soup.

3 Turn setting to high; simmer, uncovered, for 10 minutes, or until soup thickens. Serve soup in bowls, ladled over servings of rice; garnish as desired.

Serves 6 to 8

WASH-DAY STEW

SANDRA CROOK
JACKSONVILLE, FL

I was raised in rural Alabama and we had no washing machine, the only appliances we owned were a stove and refrigerator. Grandmother would do wash every Monday by building a fire, filling the old black iron pot with water and lye soap, and we would boil the clothes clean. We would then rinse and hang them up to dry. When all the work was done, this stew would be ready for Grandpa and the hungry wash women.

- **1-1/2 lb. stew beef cubes**
- **1/2 c. canned mixed vegetables**
- **1 c. water**
- **28-oz. can stewed tomatoes**
- **1 T. salt**
- **2 T. sugar**
- **1/2 c. celery, sliced**
- **1/2 c. onion, chopped**
- **2 c. potatoes, peeled and diced**
- **1 c. carrots, peeled and diced**

1 Preheat oven to 250 degrees. Place all ingredients into a greased casserole dish with a cover and bake for 3 hours.

2 Stir stew and bake for 3 hours more. Keep stew covered throughout cook time, adding additional water if needed.

Serves 6 to 8

GOOD OL' SLOPPY JOES

NANCY WYSOCK
NEW PORT RICHEY, FL

I used to take these to work and everyone loved them. They're also much requested at church potlucks.

- **1 lb. ground beef chuck**
- **1/2 c. onion, finely chopped**
- **8-oz. can tomato sauce**
- **2 T. honey**
- **1/4 t. dry mustard**
- **1/2 t. salt**
- **1/4 t. pepper**
- **4 hamburger buns or 8 slices bread**

1 Brown beef in a skillet over medium heat; drain. Add onion; cook for 3 minutes. Stir in remaining ingredients except buns or bread. Simmer for 5 minutes. Spoon onto buns or bread.

Serves 4

BONUS IDEA

Serve various kinds of chips and dips in small bowls on a big serving tray to accompany sandwiches. The kids will love it!

KEY WEST BURGERS

KIMBERLY ASCROFT
MERRITT ISLAND, FL

Dress up a plain burger with a tropical touch using slices of mango and fresh lime juice.

- **1 lb. lean ground beef**
- **3 T. Key lime juice**
- **1/4 c. fresh cilantro, chopped, divided**
- **salt and pepper to taste**
- **4 whole-wheat hamburger buns, split and toasted**
- **1 mango, pitted, peeled and sliced**
- **Garnish: lettuce**

1 In a bowl, combine beef, lime juice, 3 tablespoons cilantro, salt and pepper. Form beef mixture into 4 patties. Spray a large skillet with non-stick vegetable spray. Cook patties over medium heat for 6 minutes. Flip patties, cover skillet and cook for another 6 minutes.

2 Place lettuce on bottom halves of buns and top with patties. Add Creamy Burger Spread onto bun tops. Top with mango slices and remaining chopped cilantro. Add bun tops.

Serves 4

CREAMY BURGER SPREAD

- **1/2 c. light cream cheese, softened**
- **1/2 c. plain Greek yogurt**
- **3 green onion tops, chopped**

1 Combine all ingredients until completely blended. Cover and refrigerate at least 15 minutes.

SPINACH-CHICKEN NOODLE SOUP

ANN MAGNER
NEW PORT RICHEY, FL

Enjoy a warm bowl of this old-fashioned favorite!

- **4 14-1/4 oz. cans chicken broth**
- **1 c. onions, chopped**
- **1 c. carrots, peeled and sliced**
- **2 10-1/2 oz. cans cream of chicken soup**
- **10 oz. frozen, chopped spinach thawed**
- **4 c. cooked chicken, chopped**
- **2 c. medium egg noodles, uncooked**
- **1/2 t. salt**
- **1/2 t. pepper**

1 Combine broth, onions and carrots in Dutch oven. Bring to a boil. Cover, reduce heat; simmer for 15 minutes. Add remaining ingredients. Bring to a boil, reduce heat and simmer uncovered for 15 minutes.

Serves 10 to 12

FLORIDA FUN

You can travel around the world, gastronomically speaking, and stay in Florida the whole time. The number of ethnic influences on foods and restaurants is staggering. Here's a sampler plate of some of the main ones: Chinese, Spanish, Cuban, French, Greek, Haitian, Italian, Jamaican, Japanese, Mexican and Peruvian.

STUFFED CABBAGE SOUP

CAROLYN HELEWSKI
ARCADIA, FL

We just loved my mom's stuffed cabbage, but it took so long to prepare. I took all the ingredients she used and turned it into a soup that is a lot quicker and tastes just like the original!

1 lb. ground beef
garlic powder, salt and pepper to taste
2 14-1/2 oz. cans beef broth
3-2/3 c. water
2 10-3/4 oz. cans tomato soup
14.4-oz. can sauerkraut
1/2 head cabbage, chopped
1 c. cooked rice

1 Brown beef in a large soup pot over medium heat; drain. Sprinkle with garlic powder, salt and pepper. Add broth, water, soup and undrained sauerkraut; stir until mixed well.

2 Mix in cabbage and rice; bring to a boil. Lower heat and simmer for one hour.

Makes 10 servings

SCRAMBLED CHEESEBURGERS

WENDY MEADOWS
SPRING HILL, FL

I've been making this recipe since my kids were little. They did not like traditional hamburgers and this was more to their liking. Now it's a staple on our menu. My son will actually call me to find out what night I am making this so he can come to dinner.

1/2 to 3/4 c. onion, diced
1 lb. ground beef
Optional: garlic powder, salt and pepper to taste
4 slices American, Cheddar, Pepper Jack or Swiss cheese
4 to 6 hamburger buns, split
Garnish: favorite cheeseburger toppings

1 Add onion to a large skillet over medium heat; crumble in beef. Cook and stir, breaking up any larger pieces, until onion is translucent and beef is no longer pink. Drain.

2 Stir in garlic powder, salt and pepper, if using. Spread beef mixture into an even layer in skillet. Arrange cheese slices over beef.

3 Once the cheese starts to melt, stir it into the beef. Serve spooned onto buns; garnish with your favorite toppings.

Makes 4 to 6 servings

PROSCIUTTO BURGERS

DENISE JONES
FOUNTAIN, FL

This is a family favorite, and the prosciutto adds a deliciously different flavor to the juicy burgers.

- **1 to 1-1/2 lbs. ground beef**
- **1/2 c. dry bread crumbs**
- **1 to 2 t. dried parsley**
- **1 egg, beaten**
- **2 T. milk**
- **1/2 c. grated Parmesan cheese**
- **1/4 c. sun-dried tomatoes, chopped**
- **3/4 t. salt**
- **3/4 t. pepper**
- **6 slices prosciutto ham**
- **1/4 c. olive oil**
- **6 hamburger buns, split**
- **6 slices tomato**
- **Garnish: grated Parmesan cheese**

1 In a large bowl, mix together beef, bread crumbs, parsley, egg, milk, cheese, sun-dried tomatoes, salt and pepper.

2 Form mixture into 6 patties. Wrap each patty with a slice of prosciutto. Heat oil in a large skillet over medium heat. Fry patties in oil for 3 to 4 minutes per side, until prosciutto is crisp and burgers reach desired doneness.

3 Serve each burger in a bun, topped with a slice of tomato and sprinkled with Parmesan cheese.

Makes 6 burgers

SCARLETT'S FOOTBALL SANDWICH RING

SCARLETT HEDDEN
TITUSVILLE, FL

When we owned a deli, this was our most-requested sandwich for parties. My husband still requests it every football season. I think it's because the sandwich slices are small enough to hold in his hand. Feel free to add more meat if desired!

- **2 11-oz. tubes refrigerated crusty French loaf**
- **2 t. olive oil**
- **3 cloves garlic, pressed**
- **1/2 t. Italian seasoning**
- **1/3 c. Italian salad dressing**
- **1/3 lb. thinly sliced deli ham**
- **1/4 to 1/3 lb. thinly sliced deli turkey**
- **1/4 to 1/3 lb. thinly sliced deli roast beef**
- **1/4 lb. sliced American, Swiss or Provolone cheese, halved**
- **2 c. romaine lettuce, shredded**
- **1 red onion, thinly sliced**
- **1 green pepper, thinly sliced**
- **1 tomato, thinly sliced**
- **8 pepperoncini peppers**

1 Place both loaves of dough seam-side down on a greased 14" pizza pan, forming one large ring; pinch ends to seal. With a sharp knife, make 8 slashes, 1/2-inch deep, across top of dough.

2 Combine olive oil and garlic; lightly brush over dough. Sprinkle with Italian seasoning. Bake at 350 degrees for 25 to 30 minutes, until golden. Cool bread on pan for 10 minutes; turn out onto a wire rack and cool completely.

3 To assemble, slice bread in half horizontally. Brush cut sides with salad dressing. Layer bottom half with ham, turkey, beef, cheese, lettuce, onion, green pepper and tomato. Add top half of bread; cut into 8 sections. Top each section with a pepperoncini; fasten with a long cocktail pick, if desired. Serve immediately.

Makes 8 servings

WEEKNIGHT TREAT BURGERS

MARIE WARNER
JENNINGS, FL

My husband loves big half-pound burgers, but you could make eight smaller burgers if your family's appetites are lighter. Top these burgers with sautéed mushrooms for an extra-special meal.

1 Toss together cheese, green pepper, onion, salt and pepper in a large bowl. Add ground beef; mix well, and form into 4 patties.

2 Fry in a skillet over medium-high heat for 4 to 5 minutes on each side, or until desired doneness. Serve on rolls.

Serves 4

2/3 c. shredded provolone cheese
1/2 c. green pepper, diced
1/2 c. onion, chopped
salt and pepper to taste
2 lbs. ground beef chuck
4 sesame seed Kaiser rolls

KITCHEN TIP

Want a squeaky-clean stovetop? No elbow grease required! Cover baked-on food spots with equal parts water and baking soda and let the food soak right off.

HONEY-CHIPOTLE PULLED PORK

CAROL PATTERSON
DELTONA, FL

This slow-cooker pulled pork is easy and delicious. Chipotle peppers in adobo sauce combined with honey create a delicious sweet-heat combination that is guaranteed to be a hit!

- **3 lbs. boneless pork chops or pork roast**
- **1 c. catsup**
- **3/4 c. honey**
- **2 canned chipotle peppers in adobo sauce, chopped**
- **sliced buns**

1 Place pork in a lightly greased slow cooker. Cover and cook on low setting for 8 hours. Drain liquid and remove fat, if needed.

2 Shred pork with 2 forks. In a bowl, combine catsup, honey and chipotle peppers; pour over pork. Stir to combine; warm through. Serve on buns.

Serves 8 to 10

FLORIDA FUN

The Cuban sandwich is a classic favorite that came to Florida from Cuba, of course, in the early 1900s. It consists of roast pork, smoked ham, Swiss cheese, pickle and mustard on crusty Cuban bread. In the Miami area, some versions add salami to the sandwich, as immigrants were influenced by Italians. A bit of fusion foods, perhaps.

PEPPER STEAK SAMMIES

VICKIE
GOOSEBERRY PATCH

This is one of our favorite sandwiches! I serve this with a fresh green salad and it makes a complete meal.

- **1 to 1-1/4 lbs. beef sirloin or ribeye steak**
- **2 green peppers, thinly sliced**
- **1 onion, sliced**
- **4 cloves garlic, minced and divided**
- **1 T. oil**
- **salt and pepper to taste**
- **1/3 c. butter, softened**
- **4 French rolls, split and toasted**

1 Grill or broil steak to desired doneness; set aside. Sauté green peppers, onion and 2 cloves garlic in hot oil in a skillet over medium heat until crisp-tender; drain. Slice steak thinly; add to skillet and heat through. Sprinkle with salt and pepper.

2 Blend butter and remaining garlic; spread over cut sides of rolls. Spoon steak mixture onto bottom halves of rolls; cover with tops.

Makes 4 sandwiches

KITCHEN TIP

Keep a bottle of minced garlic on hand to save time when you're in a hurry. If swapping for fresh, remember that 1/2 teaspoon equals one clove.

BAKED CUBAN-STYLE SANDWICHES

CHERI MAXWELL
GULF BREEZE, FL

Your family & friends will love these hot, hearty sandwiches... they're just a little different!

- **2 t. honey**
- **1 t. water**
- **1 sheet frozen puff pastry dough, thawed**
- **4 t. mustard**
- **8 thin slices deli baked ham**
- **8 thin slices Swiss cheese**
- **8 thin slices deli roast pork**
- **4 sandwich-style slices kosher dill pickle**
- **2 t. sesame seed**

1 Stir together honey and water in a cup; set aside. Unfold pastry sheet on a floured surface; roll out into a 12-inch square. Cut pastry into 4, 6-inch squares. Spread each square with one teaspoon mustard, leaving a 1/2-inch border around the edge. Layer each square with 2 slices ham, 2 slices cheese, one slice pickle and 2 slices pork.

2 Brush edges of pastry with honey mixture. Fold pastry diagonally over filling to form a triangle; crimp with a fork to seal. Brush filled pastries with remaining honey mixture; sprinkle with sesame seed. Place on an ungreased baking sheet.

3 Bake at 400 degrees for 20 minutes, or until hot and golden. Set baking sheet on a wire rack for 5 minutes before serving.

Makes 4 servings

NAN'S STUFFED HOT DOGS

NANCY ROSSMAN
PORT RICHEY, FL

This simple recipe was passed down to me from my mother. We love these delicious dogs with a side of French fries or home fries. I fix two per person, but hearty eaters may want more!

16-oz. pkg. bun-length hot dogs
16-oz. can baked beans
8 long thin slices kosher dill pickle
6 slices American cheese, cut into thirds
8 slices bacon

1 Slice hot dogs lengthwise, but not all the way through. Spoon a tablespoonful of beans into each hot dog. Top with one pickle slice and 2 pieces of cheese; wrap hot dog in a bacon slice.

2 Place on a baking sheet sprayed with non-stick vegetable spray. Bake, uncovered, at 350 degrees for 30 minutes, or until bacon is crisp on top.

Makes 8 servings

KITCHEN TIP

Make biscuit toppers for bowls of thick, hearty turkey or chicken soup...they're almost like individual pot pies. Separate jumbo refrigerated biscuits, flatten them and bake according to package directions until golden. Top each soup bowl with a biscuit and dig in!

SLOW-COOKER BUTTERNUT SQUASH SOUP

BARB BARGDILL
GOOSEBERRY PATCH

I love to serve this squash soup on cold winter evenings with fresh bread and apple jelly. Yum!

2-1/2 lbs. butternut squash, halved, seeded, peeled and cubed
2 c. leeks, chopped
2 Granny Smith apples, peeled, cored and diced
2 14-1/2 oz. cans chicken broth
1 c. water
seasoned salt and white pepper to taste
Garnish: freshly ground nutmeg and sour cream

1 Combine squash, leeks, apples, broth and water in a 4-quart slow cooker. Cover and cook on high setting for 4 hours or until squash and leeks are tender.

2 Carefully purée the hot soup, in 3 or 4 batches, in a food processor or blender until smooth. Add seasoned salt and white pepper. Garnish with nutmeg and sour cream.

Serves 8

KITCHEN TIP

Use a slow cooker for dishes that you would normally cook on the stove. Try stews, chili or even chicken and noodles. It cooks by itself, so you have a little more time with family and friends.

EXTRA-CHEESY GRILLED CHEESE

BETH KRAMER
PORT SAINT LUCIE, FL

This is delicious when it is rainy or cool with a steaming bowl of tomato soup…scrumptious in summer made with produce fresh from the garden!

1/4 c. butter, softened
8 slices sourdough bread
4 slices provolone cheese
4 slices mozzarella cheese
Optional: 4 slices red onion, 4 slices tomato, 1/4 c. chopped fresh basil

1 Spread 1-1/2 teaspoons butter on each of 8 bread slices. Place one bread slice, butter-side down, in a large skillet or on a hot griddle. Layer one slice provolone and one slice mozzarella cheese on bread slice. Top with an onion slice, tomato slice and one tablespoon basil, if desired. Top with a bread slice butter-side up.

2 Reduce heat to medium-low. Cook until golden on one side, about 3 to 5 minutes; flip and cook until golden on other side. Repeat to cook remaining sandwiches.

Makes 4 sandwiches

BARBECUED HOT DOGS

NANCY MCCANN
CLEARWATER, FL

When I was a child and my mom was trying to conserve money, she would serve these hot dogs. Nowadays, my daughter is the third generation to use this recipe...it's a tasty way to dress up a pound of hot dogs. Sometimes I'll serve this on buns, sometimes not. We like to dip French fries in the sauce...yummy!

2 T. butter
1 onion, chopped
3/4 c. catsup
2 T. Worcestershire sauce
2 T. vinegar
2 T. sugar
1 t. mustard
1/2 t. paprika
1/8 t. pepper
1 lb. hot dogs, sliced lengthwise

1 Melt butter in a skillet over medium heat. Add onion and cook until transparent, about 5 minutes. Stir in remaining ingredients except hot dogs. Reduce heat and simmer for 10 minutes.

2 Place hot dogs in a lightly greased 13"x9" baking pan. Spoon sauce from skillet onto sliced hot dogs and cover with remaining sauce. Bake, uncovered, at 350 degrees for 30 minutes.

Serves 4 to 6

KITCHEN TIP

Keep vinegar handy in the kitchen for all your cleaning needs. It removes stains, sanitizes and is safe on just about any surface.

VICKIE'S SHREDDED CHICKEN SANDWICHES

VICKIE
GOOSEBERRY PATCH

Tender chicken piled high on a soft bun...just like the sandwiches at old-fashioned church socials.

1 Heat oil in a skillet over medium-high heat. Brown chicken for 5 minutes on each side. Place chicken in a slow cooker; set aside.

2 Add onion to skillet; sauté until golden. Add soup, broth, sauces, sherry or broth, salt and pepper to skillet; stir well and pour over chicken in slow cooker. Cover and cook on low setting for 6 to 8 hours. Shred chicken with a fork; spoon onto buns. Garnish with pickles and lettuce, if desired.

Makes 8 sandwiches

4 T. olive oil
4 boneless, skinless chicken breasts
1 onion, chopped
10-3/4 oz. can cream of mushroom soup
1 c. chicken broth
2 t. soy sauce
2 t. Worcestershire sauce
1/2 c. sherry or chicken broth
salt and pepper to taste
8 sandwich buns, split
Optional: pickle slices, lettuce leaves

CHAPTER FOUR

Cool & Casual

Dinnertime

WHETHER YOU PLAN TO SERVE DINNER CASUALLY FLORIDA-STYLE OR PLAN A MEAL WITH MORE SOPHISTICATED FARE, YOU'LL FIND THE PERFECT RECIPE IN THIS CHAPTER OF MAIN DISHES FOR ALL OCCASIONS.

CHICKEN PARMIGIANA

DIANE TRACY
LAKE MARY, FL

This is incredibly delicious...so tender you won't need a knife!

1 egg
3/4 c. milk
salt and pepper to taste
2 c. Italian-seasoned dry bread crumbs
4 boneless, skinless chicken breasts
2 T. oil
26-oz. jar spaghetti sauce, divided
1 to 2 c. shredded mozzarella cheese
cooked spaghetti

1 Beat together egg and milk in a deep bowl. Add salt and pepper; set aside. Place bread crumbs in a shallow bowl. Dip chicken breasts into egg mixture; coat with crumb mixture.

2 Heat oil in a skillet over medium heat; cook chicken just until golden on both sides. Add one cup sauce to bottom of a slow cooker; top with chicken. Spoon remaining sauce over chicken.

3 Cover and cook on low setting for 6 to 8 hours. About 15 minutes before serving, sprinkle cheese over top; cover until melted. Serve chicken and sauce over cooked spaghetti.

Makes 4 servings

MOMMA'S MINI MEATLOAF

KIM PAPADOPOULOS
LARGO, FL

I have made this recipe since my oldest child was little. She would help me with all the mixing...it was a fun experience for us both.

1 lb. ground beef, turkey or chicken
1 egg, beaten
1/3 c. brown sugar, packed
2 T. honey mustard
3 T. catsup
2 cloves garlic, minced
1 c. dry bread crumbs or crackers, crushed
salt and pepper to taste

1 Combine all ingredients in a large bowl; mix well. Form into 2 separate loaves and place on a greased baking sheet. May also divide into 4 mini loaf pans.

2 Bake at 350 degrees for 35 minutes, or until no longer pink in the center. To serve, cut each loaf in half.

Makes 4 servings

KITCHEN TIP

Slow cookers are so handy, you may want more than one! A 6-quart model is just right for families and potlucks, a smaller 3-quart one will cook for two and can also be used for dips and sauces.

AL'S STUFFED SHELLS

AL HAJDUCKO
HOLLYWOOD, FL

A long time ago, I made large batches of this sauce with ground beef & Italian sausage, froze it and took it to Atlanta to make the lasagna for my wedding rehearsal dinner. It's delicious and perfect for special occasions.

10 to 12 jumbo pasta shells, uncooked
16-oz. container ricotta cheese
8-oz. pkg. shredded mozzarella cheese
2 eggs, beaten
1 T. dried parsley
1 T. bacon, crisply cooked and crumbled, or real bacon bits

1 Start cooking Sauce. Cook pasta shells according to package directions, just until tender; drain.

2 Meanwhile, in a large bowl, whisk together cheeses, eggs, parsley and bacon. Spread a little Sauce in a lightly greased 13"x9" baking pan, just to cover the bottom. Spoon cheese mixture into cooked shells and arrange in pan; cover with remaining sauce. Cover with aluminum foil.

3 Bake at 350 degrees for 30 to 45 minutes, until hot and bubbly. May also divide sauce and stuffed shells between two, 9"x9" pans. Cover and freeze one pan to thaw and bake later.

Serves 4 to 6, 2 to 3 shells each

SAUCE
28-oz. can tomato purée
1/4 t. dried parsley
1/8 to 1/4 t. garlic powder
1/8 t. dried oregano
1/8 t. dried basil
1/8 t. dried marjoram
1/8 t. dried thyme
1/8 t. pepper
1 to 2 T. sugar, to taste

1 In a saucepan over medium-low heat, combine all ingredients except sugar. Cover and simmer for 15 to 20 minutes. Stir in sugar near end of cooking time; simmer 2 to 3 more minutes.

BACON FLORENTINE FETTUCCINE

BARBARA ADAMSON
OVIEDO, FL

This incredibly tasty and simple pasta dish is so fast to prepare.

- **16-oz. pkg. fettuccine pasta, uncooked**
- **2 10-oz. pkgs. frozen creamed spinach**
- **1/2 lb. bacon, crisply cooked and crumbled**
- **1/8 t. garlic powder**
- **1/2 c. plus 2 T. grated Parmesan cheese, divided**
- **pepper to taste**

1 Prepare fettuccine in a stockpot as package directs; drain, reserving 3/4 cup of cooking liquid. Microwave spinach as directed on package. Add spinach, bacon and garlic powder to stockpot.

2 Slowly drizzle reserved liquid into stockpot until sauce reaches desired consistency. Return pasta to stockpot and heat through. Transfer to a serving dish and stir in 1/2 cup cheese. Season with pepper; sprinkle with remaining cheese.

Makes 4 servings

BABA'S MEATBALLS

CAROL GEYER
PORT CHARLOTTE, FL

This is a recipe from my Baba, as we called my grandmother. She knew all the old Slovakian ways of making food stretch.

- **3 slices white bread**
- **3 lbs. ground beef**
- **2 eggs, beaten**
- **1 onion, chopped**
- **1/4 c. fresh parsley, chopped**
- **1 c. milk**
- **5 potatoes, peeled and halved**
- **5 stalks celery, halved lengthwise**
- **2 to 3 T. butter, thinly sliced**
- **pepper to taste**

1 Let bread slices stand at room temperature for 2 hours, until slightly dry. Combine beef, eggs, onion and parsley in a large bowl; set aside. Tear bread into bite-size pieces. Dip bread in milk and add to beef mixture, blending well.

2 Form into baseball-size balls; place in an ungreased roasting pan. Add potatoes; place celery across meatballs and potatoes. Dot meatballs with butter; sprinkle with pepper. Bake, covered, at 350 degrees for 2 hours, or until meatballs are cooked through and vegetables are tender.

Serves 4 to 6

FLORIDA FUN

You might be hard-pressed to create a revered Southern fried chicken recipe. But Publix, a grocery store chain, wasn't. Its take-out fried chicken, right next to the deli department in its stores, has legions and legions of followers.

CHICKEN BACON-RANCH BAKE

NICOLE MANLEY
JACKSONVILLE, FL

I started dieting but love comfort foods, so I set out to create that feeling. This is one of the recipes I came up with that my whole family loves. Each portion is under 400 calories!

12-oz. pkg. frozen cauliflower

1/2 lb. boneless, skinless chicken breast, cooked and cubed

1 bunch green onions, chopped

2 T. light ranch salad dressing

1-1/2 c. shredded Colby-Jack cheese, divided

salt and pepper to taste

2 slices bacon, crisply cooked and crumbled

1 Cook cauliflower according to package directions; drain very well. In a bowl, combine cauliflower, chicken, green onions, salad dressing, 1-1/4 cups cheese, salt and pepper. Mix well; spoon into an 8"x8" baking pan sprayed with non-stick vegetable spray. Sprinkle bacon and remaining cheese on top.

2 Cover and bake at 350 degrees for 30 minutes, or until heated through and cheese is melted.

Makes 4 servings

LEMONADE CHICKEN

KATHY WERNER
MINNEOLA, FL

Everyone loves this chicken! My girls are now on their own, and this is one of the first recipes I gave them.

- **6 skinless chicken thighs**
- **1/2 c. all-purpose flour**
- **1 t. salt**
- **1 to 2 T. oil**
- **6-oz. can frozen lemonade concentrate**
- **3 T. brown sugar, packed**
- **3 T. catsup**
- **1 t. balsamic vinegar or cider vinegar**
- **2 T. cornstarch**
- **1/4 c. cold water**

1 Dredge chicken in flour mixed with salt. In a skillet over medium heat, cook chicken in oil until golden; drain. Transfer chicken to a slow cooker. Mix lemonade, brown sugar, catsup and vinegar; pour over chicken.

2 Cover and cook on low setting for 6 to 8 hours, or on high setting for 3 to 4 hours. Remove chicken to a platter; keep warm. Whisk cornstarch into cold water; add to juices in slow cooker. Cover and cook on high setting to desired sauce consistency, about 15 minutes. Serve chicken with sauce.

Makes 6 servings

Key Lime Cupcakes, p.133

Whether you are looking for a quick-to-make breakfast dish to start the day off right, no-fuss party fare for those special guests, satisfying soups and sandwiches for the perfect lunch, main dishes to bring them to the table fast, or a sweet little something to savor at the end of the meal, you'll love these recipes from the amazing cooks in the beautiful state of Florida.

Mandarin Orange Salad, p.35

Rosemary-Lemon-Pineapple Punch, p.113

Twice-Baked Sweet Potato, p.42
Apple & Brie Toasts, p.110
Bacon Florentine Fettuccine, p.77
Chicken & Rice Salad, p.27

Chocolate-Hazelnut Skillet Bars, p.131

Chunky Tomato-Avocado Salad, p.31

Dad's Famous Minestrone, p.47

Cheesy Chicken & Broccoli Rice Bowls, p.91

Black Bean Breakfast Bowls, p.13

Baja Shrimp Quesadillas, p.89

Blueberry Cream Pie, p.132

Herb Garden Chicken, p.99

Inside-Out Ravioli, p.101

Julie's Strawberry Yum-Yum, p.135

Garden Patch Grilled Vegetables, p.29

Mom's Cola Chicken, p.107

Roasted Tomato-Feta Broccoli, p.42

Shrimp Tossed Salad, p.41

Pumpkin Patch Cheese Ball, p.120

Herbed Mushroom Omelets, p.17

Spinach & Tomato French Toast, p.20

Marianne's Cranberry Roll-Ups, p.114

Key West Burgers, p.57

Turkey Fruit Salad, p.37

Crustless Coconut Pie, p.140

BAJA SHRIMP QUESADILLAS

JOANN
GOOSEBERRY PATCH

These quesadillas are always a special treat with all the yummy ingredients inside each tasty little serving. I serve them with a green salad for a meal or cut them smaller for appetizers.

2-1/2 lbs. shrimp, peeled and cleaned
3 c. shredded Cheddar cheese
1/2 c. mayonnaise
3/4 c. salsa
1/4 t. ground cumin
1/4 t. cayenne pepper
1/4 t. pepper
12 6-inch flour tortillas
Garnish: plain Greek yogurt, chopped fresh parsley

1 Chop shrimp, discarding tails. Mix shrimp, cheese, mayonnaise, salsa, cumin and peppers; spread one to 2 tablespoons on one tortilla. Place another tortilla on top; put on a greased baking sheet. Repeat with remaining tortillas.

2 Bake at 350 degrees for 15 minutes; remove and cut into triangles. Garnish as desired.

Serves 12

BELA'S FAVORITE PASTA FAGIOLI

JULIE DOSSANTOS
FORT PIERCE, FL

Our daughter Bela adores this slow-cooker soup recipe. It is the most requested recipe in our home throughout the year. Simple to make and delicious any night of the week...we like to serve this soup with slices of crusty Italian bread.

1 t. olive oil
2 14-1/2 oz. cans Italian-style diced tomatoes
2 15-oz. cans cannellini beans, drained and rinsed
2 cloves garlic, diced
1/2 c. fresh basil, chopped
2 T. Italian seasoning
1-1/2 t. salt
1 t. pepper
2 32-oz. containers chicken or vegetable broth
16-oz. pkg. ditalini pasta, cooked
Garnish: thinly sliced mozzarella cheese

1 Combine oil, undrained tomatoes, beans, garlic, basil and seasonings in a slow cook; mix well. Add broth; stir.

2 Cover and cook on low setting for 6 hours. Divide pasta among soup bowls; ladle soup over pasta. Garnish each bowl with a slice of mozzarella cheese.

Serves 6 to 8

CHEESY CHICKEN & BROCCOLI RICE BOWLS

SARA JACKSON
TAMPA, FL

This was one of the first dishes I learned how to make. It's still a favorite!

- 3 c. broccoli, chopped
- 1 T. olive oil
- 1/2 lb. boneless, skinless chicken breast, cubed
- 1/4 t. salt
- 1/4 t. pepper
- 1/2 c. green onions, chopped
- 1 c. shredded mild Cheddar cheese
- 2 c. cooked brown rice, warmed
- 2 T. toasted sliced almonds

1 In a saucepan over medium heat, cook broccoli with a small amount of water until tender; drain and set aside.

2 Meanwhile, heat oil in a skillet over medium-high heat. Add chicken; season with salt and pepper. Cook until tender and chicken juices run clear. Add onions and cheese; cook and stir until cheese melts. Fold in cooked rice and broccoli. Cook for one to 2 minutes, until heated through.

3 To serve, divide among 4 bowls; top with almonds.

Makes 4 servings

EASY POACHED SALMON

JO ANN
GOOSEBERRY PATCH

An elegant dinner for guests...or treat your family! I like to serve tender roasted asparagus with this salmon.

1 c. water
1/2 c. white wine or vegetable broth
1/2 c. onion, sliced
2 sprigs fresh parsley, snipped
5 peppercorns
1/4 t. salt
1 lb. salmon fillets

1 In a one-quart microwave-safe dish, combine all ingredients except fish; stir well. Cover with plastic wrap. Microwave on high for 2 to 3 minutes, until mixture boils. Discard peppercorns, if desired.

2 Place fish in a separate microwave-safe dish. Pour mixture over fish. Cover and microwave on medium-high for 5 to 6 minutes, until fish flakes easily with a fork. Carefully remove fish to a serving plate. Serve immediately, or chill and serve cold. Serve with Creamy Dijon Sauce.

Makes 4 servings

CREAMY DIJON SAUCE

1/2 c. sour cream
1 T. Dijon mustard
1 T. lemon juice
2 t. fresh dill, chopped

1 Combine all ingredients; mix well and chill before serving

COZY CHICKEN & NOODLES

SARAH ZAOUZAL
CLERMONT, FL

I make this simple, creamy skillet recipe for my family all the time. Everyone always asks for seconds, even picky toddlers...serve it and just watch it disappear!

1 onion, chopped
1/2 c. fresh flat-leaf parsley, chopped
2 to 3 t. margarine
salt, pepper and onion powder to taste
4 boneless, skinless chicken breasts
10-3/4 oz. can cream of mushroom soup
1 c. milk
8-oz. pkg. wide egg noodles, uncooked

1 In a large deep skillet over medium heat, sauté onion and parsley in margarine until onion is softened. Season with salt, pepper and onion powder.

2 Sauté chicken breasts until golden on both sides; cut into bite-size pieces. Add more salt, pepper and onion powder to chicken, if desired. Continue cooking until chicken is almost cooked through. Stir in soup and milk; bring to a boil.

3 Reduce heat to low and simmer for 30 minutes, stirring occasionally. Meanwhile, cook noodles according to package directions; drain. To serve, ladle chicken mixture over noodles.

Makes 4 servings

EASY SKILLET SHRIMP

CHERI MAXWELL
GULF BREEZE, FL

Ready in a flash! Serve over angel hair pasta and add a sprinkle of chopped fresh parsley.

- **1 lb. uncooked large shrimp, peeled and cleaned**
- **2 t. seafood seasoning**
- **1 T. butter or olive oil**

1 Sprinkle shrimp with seasoning; toss to coat well and set aside. Heat butter or oil in a skillet over medium-high heat. Add shrimp. Cook for 3 to 5 minutes, stirring occasionally, until pink.

Serves 4

FLORIDA FUN

Stone crab claws, served cold with mustard sauce for dipping, have lots of die-hard fans. They might suggest Joe's Stone Crab in Miami Beach, which has been said to be the first place to serve it.

EASY SMOTHERED CHICKEN

LISA JOHNSON
TRENTON, FL

I came up with this dish for work one day and it was a hit...really scrumptious!

4 boneless, skinless chicken breasts
1 c. zesty Italian salad dressing
8 slices smoked bacon
4 slices Colby cheese, or 1 c. shredded Colby cheese

1 Pound chicken with a meat mallet until slightly flattened. Place chicken in a large plastic zipping bag; cover with salad dressing. Seal bag and refrigerate for 2 to 4 hours. Remove chicken from bag, discarding dressing.

2 Wrap 2 slices of bacon around each chicken piece. Spray a countertop grill with non-stick vegetable spray. Place chicken on preheated grill. Cook for about 5 to 10 minutes, until bacon is crisp and chicken juices run clear. Remove chicken to a baking pan; top with cheese.

3 Bake, uncovered, at 350 degrees for 3 to 5 minutes, until cheese is melted.

Makes 4 servings

GARDEN-STYLE CHEESY HASHBROWN BAKE

BETH KRAMER
PORT SAINT LUCIE, FL

We all love our cheesy hashbrowns! This casserole is packed with fresh veggies so it's colorful and good for you. Finely chopped broccoli would be delicious too.

- **2 T. butter**
- **2 c. frozen diced potatoes, thawed**
- **1/2 lb. fresh asparagus, diced**
- **1/2 lb. sliced mushrooms**
- **1 red pepper, diced**
- **1 green pepper, diced**
- **1/2 c. onion, diced**
- **1 doz. eggs**
- **1/3 c. sour cream**
- **8-oz. pkg. pasteurized process cheese slices**

1 Melt butter in a large skillet over medium-high heat; add vegetables. Cook for 10 minutes, stirring often, until tender.

2 Spread mixture in a 13"x9" baking pan sprayed with non-stick vegetable spray. In a large bowl, whisk eggs and sour cream until blended; pour over vegetable mixture. Top with cheese. Bake, uncovered, at 350 degrees for 40 minutes, or until vegetables are tender and center is set. Let stand several minutes; cut into squares.

Makes 12 servings

EASY THANKSGIVING DINNER

MATT MCCURDY
SAINT PETERSBURG, FL

Simply toss everything in the slow cooker, and you have a scrumptious turkey dinner with all the trimmings...doesn't get much easier than that!

1 T. oil
2-lb. boneless, skinless turkey breast
12-oz. pkg. favorite-flavor stuffing mix
1 sweet potato, peeled and cubed
1/2 c. celery, chopped
1/2 c. onion, chopped
1/2 c. carrot, peeled and chopped
2 c. chicken broth
1/2 c. chopped walnuts
1/2 c. fresh cranberries

1 Heat oil in a skillet over medium heat. Sauté turkey in oil until browned on both sides, about 5 minutes; drain. Combine turkey and remaining ingredients except nuts and cranberries in a slow cooker.

2 Cover and cook on low setting for 7 to 8 hours, or until turkey is no longer pink in the center. About one hour before serving, stir in walnuts and cranberries.

Serves 6 to 8

FLORIDA FUN

'Gator tails and 'gator bites might have appeal to some adventurous tourists. Do they taste like chicken?

GRAMMY'S TRIO PASTA

MARIA MAXEY
DAVENPORT, FL

This quick & delicious pasta salad is a must at cookouts and picnics. The dressing tastes wonderful on salads and Italian sandwiches too!

12-oz. box tri-color rotini pasta, uncooked
1 red pepper, chopped
1 green pepper, chopped
1 zucchini, chopped
8-oz. can sliced black olives, drained
1 red onion, chopped
1 c. cherry tomatoes, halved
8-oz. pkg. crumbled feta cheese
Garnish: fresh basil leaves

1 Cook pasta according to package directions; drain and rinse with cold water. Combine all ingredients except feta cheese and garnish in a large bowl; toss to mix well.

2 Pour Pasta Salad Dressing over mixture; stir to coat well. Fold in feta cheese; garnish with basil.

Makes 10 to 12 servings

PASTA SALAD DRESSING

1/2 c. extra-virgin olive oil
1/3 c. cider vinegar
2 T. balsamic vinegar
2 T. honey
2 T. Italian seasoning
1 t. red pepper flakes
1/4 t. cayenne pepper
1/2 t. sea salt

1 Whisk together all ingredients in a bowl.

HERB GARDEN CHICKEN

JULIE NEFF
CITRUS SPRINGS, FL

This is the chicken dish my husband asks for most often. I'm happy to oblige because it's so tasty and so easy to put together.

- 4 to 6 boneless, skinless chicken breasts
- 2 tomatoes, chopped
- 1 onion, chopped
- 2 cloves garlic, chopped
- 2/3 c. chicken broth
- 1 bay leaf
- 1 t. dried thyme
- 1-1/2 t. salt
- 1 t. pepper, or more to taste
- 2 c. broccoli flowerets
- Optional: 2 to 3 T. all-purpose flour
- cooked rice

1 Place chicken in a slow cooker; top with tomatoes, onion and garlic. In a bowl, combine broth and seasonings; pour over chicken mixture.

2 Cover and cook on low setting for 8 hours. Add broccoli; cook for one additional hour, or until chicken juices run clear and broccoli is tender. Juices in slow cooker may be thickened with flour, if desired. Discard bay leaf; serve chicken and vegetables over cooked rice.

Makes 4 to 6 servings

KITCHEN TIP

A flexible plastic cutting mat makes speedy work of slicing & dicing. Keep two mats on hand for chopping meat and veggies separately.

MY FAVORITE ONE-POT MEAL

LIZ PLOTNICK-SNAY
GOOSEBERRY PATCH

Curry powder, raisins and chopped apple make this chicken dish just a little different.

- **2 onions, diced**
- **1/4 c. oil, divided**
- **2-1/2 to 3 lbs. boneless, skinless chicken breasts**
- **14-1/2 oz. can diced tomatoes**
- **1/2 c. white wine or chicken broth**
- **1 T. curry powder**
- **1/4 t. garlic powder**
- **1/4 t. dried thyme**
- **1/4 t. nutmeg**
- **1 apple, peeled, cored and cubed**
- **1/4 c. raisins**
- **3 T. whipping cream**
- **1/2 t. lemon juice**
- **2 c. cooked rice**

1 Sauté onions in 2 tablespoons oil over medium heat in a large skillet; remove onions and set aside. Add remaining oil and chicken to skillet; cook chicken until golden.

2 Return onions to skillet; add tomatoes, wine or broth and spices. Mix well; reduce heat, cover and simmer for 20 minutes. Add apple, raisins and cream; simmer over low heat for an additional 6 to 8 minutes. Stir in lemon juice. Serve over cooked rice.

Makes 3 to 4 servings

INSIDE-OUT RAVIOLI

JO ANN
GOOSEBERRY PATCH

Just add a crisp tossed salad with oil & vinegar dressing for a hearty Italian-style meal. Please pass the Parmesan!

16-oz. pkg. small shell or bowtie pasta, uncooked
1 lb. ground beef
1 c. onion, chopped
1/2 c. dry bread crumbs
1 egg, beaten
1 t. Italian seasoning
1 t. salt
1 t. pepper
8-oz. pkg. sliced mushrooms
10-oz. pkg. frozen chopped spinach, thawed and drained
16-oz. jar spaghetti sauce
1 c. shredded mozzarella cheese
Garnish: grated Parmesan cheese

1 Cook pasta according to package directions; drain. Meanwhile, brown beef with onion in a skillet over medium heat; drain. In a greased 13"x9" baking pan, combine cooked pasta, beef mixture and remaining ingredients except sauce and cheeses. Stir gently; top with sauce and mozzarella cheese.

2 Bake, uncovered, at 350 degrees for 45 minutes, or until hot and bubbly. Sprinkle with Parmesan cheese at serving time.

Makes 10 servings

MEATLOAF MEXICANA

JO ANN
GOOSEBERRY PATCH

I like to serve this tasty dish alongside some zesty refried beans and a warm slice of cornbread. We also like to have a nice green salad with this rich meatloaf to round out the meal. So yummy!

1 lb. ground pork
3/4 lb. lean ground beef
1 c. shredded low-fat Monterey Jack cheese, divided
1 c. dry bread crumbs
1/2 c. taco sauce
2 eggs, beaten
1 T. fresh parsley, chopped
2 t. canned diced jalapeño peppers
Garnish: chopped tomatoes, sliced green onions

1 Combine meats, 3/4 cup cheese and remaining ingredients except garnish in a large bowl. Gently press into a lightly greased 9"x5" loaf pan.

2 Bake, uncovered at 350 degrees for 55 to 60 minutes, until no longer pink in center. Top with remaining cheese; garnish as desired.

Makes 8 servings

CROCKERY CHICKEN PARMIGIANA

DIANE TRACY
LAKE MARY, FL

This chicken is incredibly delicious and so tender you won't need a knife. Everyone is incredulous...chicken parmigiana in the slow cooker? Then they try it and they are sold!

1 egg
1/2 c. milk
salt and pepper to taste
1 to 1-1/2 c. Italian-flavored dry bread crumbs
1/2 t. garlic powder
1/2 t. dried oregano
1/2 t. dried basil
4 boneless, skinless chicken breasts
2 T. oil
26-oz. jar spaghetti sauce, divided
1 c. shredded mozzarella cheese

1 Whisk together egg and milk in a shallow bowl; sprinkle with salt and pepper. In a separate shallow bowl, combine bread crumbs and seasonings. Dip each piece of chicken in egg mixture, then dredge in bread crumb mixture until well coated.

2 In a skillet over medium heat, brown chicken in oil until crust is deeply golden. Do not cook through. Spread one cup sauce in a slow cooker; add chicken. Top with remaining sauce.

3 Cover and cook on low setting for 6 to 8 hours. About 15 minutes before serving, sprinkle with cheese. Cover and cook on low setting for 15 minutes, or until cheese melts.

Serves 4

BUTTER-BAKED CHICKEN

ELLEN FOLKMAN
CRYSTAL BEACH, FL

My husband loves this recipe. It's warm and comforting on a cool fall or winter night. Mashed potatoes are a must...the gravy is delicious!

1/4 c. butter, sliced
1 c. all-purpose flour
1 t. salt
1/2 t. pepper
12-oz. can evaporated milk, divided
4 chicken breasts
10-3/4 oz. can cream of chicken soup
1/4 c. water

1 Place butter in a 13"x9" baking pan; melt in a 350-degree oven and set aside.

2 Meanwhile, in a shallow bowl, combine flour, salt and pepper. Add 1/2 cup evaporated milk to a separate shallow bowl. Dip chicken pieces in milk; dredge in flour mixture. Arrange chicken, skin-side up, in baking pan.

3 Bake, uncovered, at 350 degrees for 35 minutes. In a small bowl, combine soup, water and remaining milk. Turn chicken over; spoon soup mixture over chicken. Bake an additional 35 minutes, or until chicken is no longer pink. Remove chicken to a serving platter. Whisk gravy in pan until smooth. Spoon gravy over chicken; serve any remaining gravy on the side.

Serves 4

CRISPY TILAPIA

SCARLETT HEDDEN
TITUSVILLE, FL

Living in Florida presents the opportunity to try out all kinds of fish! When my husband goes fishing you can be assured we'll have lots of tilapia. This is my favorite recipe because it is low-calorie and has just a few ingredients. I like to use Italian panko bread crumbs because they make a crispier fish with more flavor.

1 c. Italian-seasoned panko bread crumbs
1/2 c. grated Parmesan cheese
1 t. garlic powder
Optional: 1/2 t. red pepper flakes
4 5-oz. tilapia fillets
Optional: chunky salsa

1 In a shallow bowl, combine bread crumbs, cheese, garlic powder and red pepper flakes, if using. Press fish fillets into crumb mixture to coat well on both sides. Arrange on a baking sheet sprayed with non-stick vegetable spray.

2 Bake at 425 degrees for 12 minutes, or until fish flakes easily with a fork. If desired, serve with a spoonful of chunky salsa spooned over each fillet.

Makes 4 servings

CRUNCHY CORN CHIP CHICKEN

TEGAN REEVES
AUBURNDALE, FL

So quick to whip up!

- **5 boneless, skinless chicken breasts**
- **10-3/4 oz. can cream of chicken soup**
- **2 c. shredded Cheddar cheese, divided**
- **1-1/4 oz. pkg. taco seasoning mix**
- **2 c. barbecue corn chips, crushed**

1 Arrange chicken in an ungreased 13"x9" baking pan; set aside. Combine soup, one cup cheese and taco seasoning together; spread over chicken.

2 Bake at 450 degrees for 45 minutes; sprinkle with corn chips and remaining cheese. Return to oven; bake until cheese melts, about 5 minutes.

Makes 6 servings

FLORIDA FUN

Stop at any seafood shack, and there are many, and you'll find many kinds of fish...from fried or broiled to blackened or grilled. Take your pick!

MOM'S COLA CHICKEN

CARLA SLAJCHERT
SAINT PETERSBURG, FL

Growing up, we knew Mom would be making this delicious, tender chicken whenever we saw her get out the electric skillet.

1 to 2 T. oil
1-1/2 lbs. boneless, skinless chicken breasts
salt and pepper to taste
20-oz. bottle cola, divided
1 to 2 c. catsup, divided

1 Heat oil in a large skillet over medium heat. Add chicken to oil; sprinkle with salt and pepper and brown on both sides. Pour enough cola into skillet to cover chicken. Slowly add enough catsup to skillet until mixture reaches desired thicknesss.

2 Cover and cook over medium heat for about 45 minutes, adding remaining cola and catsup, a little at a time, every 10 to 15 minutes, until chicken juices run clear.

Serves 4

CHAPTER FIVE

No-Fuss Snacks & Appetizers

WHETHER YOU ARE HAVING A SPECIAL PARTY OR JUST NEED A LITTLE SNACK TO TIDE YOU OVER TO THE NEXT MEAL, THESE RECIPES ARE SURE TO BECOME YOUR FAVORITE GO-TO GOODIES.

MARIE'S BLACK BEAN DIP

MARIE STEWART
FORT WALTON BEACH, FL

Good! good! good! When I am really rushed, but need something everyone loves, I go for this appetizer. It's so good I always make copies of the recipe for those who request it.

- **2 8-oz. pkgs. cream cheese, softened**
- **15-1/2 oz. can black beans, drained and rinsed**
- **10-oz. can diced tomatoes with green chiles, drained**
- **2 T. taco seasoning mix**
- **tortilla chips**

1 In a large bowl, combine all ingredients except chips; mix well. Cover and refrigerate at least 2 hours. Serve with tortilla chips.

Makes 10 to 12 servings

APPLE & BRIE TOASTS

JO ANN
GOOSEBERRY PATCH

These little tidbits of flavor are so showy and easy to make. We make them often!

- **1 baguette, cut into 1/4-inch-thick slices**
- **1/4 c. brown sugar, packed**
- **1/4 c. chopped walnuts**
- **3 T. butter, melted**
- **13.2-oz. pkg. Brie cheese, thinly sliced**
- **3 Granny Smith apples and/or Braeburn apples, cored and sliced**

1 Arrange baguette slices on an ungreased baking sheet; bake at 350 degrees until lightly toasted. Set aside. Mix together brown sugar, walnuts and butter.

2 Top each slice of bread with a cheese slice, an apple slice and 1/2 teaspoon of brown sugar mixture. Bake at 350 degrees until cheese melts, 2 to 4 minutes.

Makes 2-1/2 dozen

GARDEN-FRESH SHRIMP SALSA

JULIE HUTSON
CALLAHAN, FL

Great with baked crackers or as a topping for bruschetta.

- **1 lb. cooked shrimp, peeled and chopped**
- **4 ripe tomatoes, diced**
- **1/4 c. red onion, finely diced**
- **1 jalapeño pepper, finely diced, seeds removed**
- **2 T. fresh cilantro, finely chopped**
- **juice of 3 limes**
- **1 T. sea salt**

1 In a glass or plastic bowl, toss together all ingredients except lime juice and salt; mix well. Stir in lime juice and salt, adding more or less of both to taste.

2 Cover and refrigerate at least one hour before serving.

Serves 8

PEPPER CORN CUPS

KIMBERLY ASCROFT
MERRITT ISLAND, FL

I first made this appetizer for a Christmas party. It has turned into an anytime favorite!

- **8-oz. round Brie cheese**
- **16-oz. pkg. frozen corn, thawed**
- **1 red pepper, diced**
- **1 orange pepper, diced**
- **3 2-oz. pkgs. frozen mini phyllo shells, thawed**

1 Trim and discard rind from Brie; cut Brie into cubes. Mix together corn and peppers. Place mini phyllo shells on lightly greased baking sheets; evenly divide corn mixture into shells. Place one cube of Brie on each shell.

2 Bake at 350 degrees for 5 to 8 minutes.

Makes 3-3/4 dozen

CARAMEL-CINNAMON GRAHAM CRACKERS

JO ANN
GOOSEBERRY PATCH

Such an easy treat to whip up when you just need a little something!

- **24 cinnamon graham crackers, divided**
- **1/2 c. butter, softened**
- **1/2 c. margarine, softened**
- **1 c. light brown sugar, packed**
- **1 c. chopped pecans**

1 Arrange a single layer of graham crackers on an aluminum foil-lined 15"x10" jelly-roll pan. Set aside. In a saucepan over medium-low heat, combine butter, margarine and brown sugar. Bring to a boil; cook for 2 minutes. Stir well and pour over crackers. Sprinkle nuts on top. Bake at 350 degrees for 12 minutes. Cut into triangles.

Makes 4 dozen

CELEBRATION PARTY MIX

FRANCES CLICK
HERNANDO BEACH, FL

We serve this snack mix on many occasions. My husband loves it and is always looking for a reason to celebrate! Just change the color of the candy-coated milk chocolate pieces to suit the occasion.

- **2 c. bite-size crispy corn cereal squares**
- **2 c. mini pretzels**
- **1 c. cocktail peanuts**
- **1 c. candy-coated chocolates**
- **12-oz. pkg white chocolate chips**

1 In a large bowl, combine all ingredients except chocolate chips; toss to mix and set aside. Place chocolate chips in a microwave-safe bowl. Microwave for one minute; stir. Microwave again as needed, 15 seconds at a time, until melted. Stir chocolate until smooth. Pour over cereal mixture; toss to coat.

2 Immediately pour onto wax paper-lined baking sheets; spread out. Let stand until chocolate is set, about 20 minutes. Break into pieces. Store in an airtight container.

Makes about 8 cups

ROSEMARY-LEMON-PINEAPPLE PUNCH

CHERI MAXWELL
GULF BREEZE, FL

A refreshing beverage that's perfect for a garden party or reception.

46-oz. can unsweetened pineapple juice
1-1/2 c. lemon juice
2 c. water
3/4 to 1 c. sugar
4 to 5 sprigs fresh rosemary
1-ltr. bottle ginger ale, chilled
Garnish: fresh pineapple slices, fresh rosemary sprigs

1 Combine juices, water, sugar and rosemary in a large saucepan over medium heat. Bring to a boil. Stir until sugar dissolves.

2 Remove from heat; cover and let stand for 15 minutes. Discard rosemary; chill. Before serving, add ginger ale; serve immediately. Garnish as desired.

Serves 12

CHEESY BRUSCHETTA

SCARLETT HEDDEN
TITUSVILLE, FL

Oh, yum...this simple little recipe is so darn good! Easy to make and great for football parties or when you need a deelish appetizer.

1/2 c. grated Parmesan cheese
1/4 c. red onion or green onions, finely chopped
1/2 c. mayonnaise
1 long thin French loaf, sliced 1/4 to 1/2-inch thick

1 Combine cheese, onion and mayonnaise in a small bowl; mix well. Spread one tablespoon of mixture on each bread slice; cut each slice in half. Arrange on ungreased baking sheets.

2 Bake at 350 degrees until bubbly and golden, about 8 to 10 minutes, watching closely to avoid burning.

Makes 12 to 15 servings

CREAMY SPINACH & ONION DIP

JANIS GREENE
BRANDON, FL

This is my favorite dip...it's a big hit at every party!

- 3 8-oz. pkgs. cream cheese, softened
- 2 c. shredded Italian-blend cheese
- 10-oz. pkg. frozen chopped spinach, thawed and well drained
- 10-oz. pkg. frozen chopped onions, thawed and well drained
- 3-oz. pkg. bacon crumbles
- crackers or chips

1 In a large bowl, combine all ingredients except chips or crackers; mix well. Spoon mixture into a lightly greased 2-quart casserole dish.

2 Bake, uncovered, at 350 degrees for 30 minutes, or until hot and bubbly. Serve warm with crackers or chips.

Makes 20 servings

MARIANNE'S CRANBERRY ROLL-UPS

SANDI GIVERSON
VERO BEACH, FL

One of the girls I work with, Marianne Hudgins, always has the best recipes! With her permission, here is one of my favorites.

- 8-oz. container light whipped cream cheese
- 8-oz. pkg. crumbled feta cheese
- 6-oz. pkg. dried cranberries
- 3 T. fresh chives, chopped
- 4 10-inch whole-grain flour tortillas

1 Combine all ingredients except tortillas together; blend until smooth. Spread mixture over tortillas, roll up and wrap in plastic wrap; chill until ready to serve. Cut each roll into one-inch slices.

Serves 10

GRANDMA LIND'S FUDGE

ADONNA MULLEN
PANAMA CITY, FL

This recipe was my grandmother's favorite. I remember staying with her when I was a little girl and I would get so excited to help Granny make her fudge. Granny always eyeballed everything and used a pinch of this & that. She has been gone for 15 years now. When I think of her, I always make a pan of her delicious fudge.

1 c. creamy peanut butter
1/2 c. butter
3/4 c. milk
2-1/2 c. sugar
1/2 c. baking cocoa
1 T. corn syrup
1/8 t. salt
1 t. vanilla extract
Optional: 1 c. chopped walnuts

1 Prepare a lightly buttered 9"x9" baking pan; set aside. Place peanut butter and butter on a saucer; set aside. In a large heavy saucepan over medium-high heat, combine milk, sugar, cocoa, corn syrup and salt.

2 Cook, stirring constantly, until mixture starts to boil and reaches the soft-ball stage, or 234 to 243 degrees on a candy thermometer. Remove from heat; stir in vanilla, peanut butter, butter and walnuts, if using. Beat by hand until mixture thickens; pour into pan. Let stand until set; cut into small squares.

Makes about 3 dozen

PEANUT BUTTER FUDGE

Simply omit baking cocoa from above recipe.

CROWD-PLEASIN' CHUTNEY SPREAD

GINA MCCLENNING
BROOKSVILLE, FL

Why is it that anything with bacon in it is so darn good? This is one of those spreads that is always a hit at parties!

- **2 8-oz. pkgs. light cream cheese, softened**
- **3 T. curry powder**
- **1 t. salt**
- **5-oz. jar ginger chutney or other favorite chutney**
- **2 bunches green onions, sliced**
- **10 slices bacon, crisply cooked and crumbled**
- **1/4 c. almonds, finely chopped**
- **Melba toast or wheat crackers**

1 In a bowl, combine cream cheese and seasonings. Blend well; spread in the bottom of a 10" quiche dish. Purée chutney in a food processor or blender.

2 Spread chutney over cheese mixture. Sprinkle evenly with onions, bacon and almonds. Serve immediately, or cover and refrigerate up to a day ahead. Serve with Melba toast or wheat crackers.

Serves 8

HOMEMADE CARAMEL CORN

SOPHIA GRAVES
OKEECHOBEE, FL

A lady I work with made this recipe for a fundraiser and when I tasted it, this brought back such memories of Halloween past. Fall carnivals always used to sell caramel corn...it was a treat we only received once a year. Once you start eating, it is really hard to stop!

16 c. popped corn
1-1/2 c. salted peanuts
1-1/2 c. sugar
3/4 c. butter, sliced
1/2 c. dark corn syrup
1 t. vanilla extract
1/2 t. baking soda

1 Place popcorn in a roaster pan; discard any unpopped kernels. Sprinkle peanuts evenly over the top; set aside. In a heavy saucepan over medium heat, combine sugar, butter, corn syrup and vanilla.

2 Bring to a boil while stirring. Reduce heat until simmering. Continue cooking and stirring until a caramel color appears. Remove from heat; stir in baking soda.

3 Pour sugar mixture over popcorn mixture; stir with a large spoon until coated. Bake, uncovered, at 250 degrees for one hour, stirring every 15 minutes. Cool before serving. Store in a covered container.

Makes 18 cups

JAN'S CHEESE BALLS

JOANN
GOOSEBERRY PATCH

I found this recipe in a local church cookbook published about the same time Gooseberry Patch was founded. It's still very tasty!

- **3 8-oz. pkgs. cream cheese, softened**
- **2 5-oz. jars sharp cheese spread**
- **5-oz. jar blue cheese spread**
- **1-1/2 t. Worcestershire sauce**
- **garlic salt to taste**
- **1/4 t. pepper**
- **Garnish: chopped nuts or chopped fresh parsley**

1 Combine all cheeses in a large bowl. Cover; let stand at room temperature until softened. Beat well with an electric mixer on medium-low speed. Beat in Worcestershire sauce and seasonings.

2 Cover and refrigerate overnight to allow flavors to blend. Shape cheese mixture into 2 or more balls; roll in chopped nuts or parsley to coat. Wrap again and chill until serving time.

Serves 10 to 12

TIME-OUT CHICKEN WINGS

DARRELL LAWRY
KISSIMMEE, FL

An oldie but goodie that I just rediscovered...it's too good to forget!

- **3 lbs. chicken wings, separated**
- **8-oz. bottle Catalina salad dressing**
- **1/4 c. soy sauce**
- **2 t. fresh ginger, peeled and minced**

1 Place chicken wings in a large plastic zipping bag; set aside. Combine remaining ingredients; pour over wings. Seal bag and refrigerate several hours to overnight. Drain; bring marinade to a boil in a small saucepan.

2 Place wings on a broiler pan. Broil for about 20 minutes, turning once, until chicken juices run clear. Brush occasionally with marinade.

Makes about 3 dozen

NAN'S CHIPPED BEEF & PIMENTO CHEESE BALL

NANCY ROSSMAN
PORT RICHEY, FL

I bring this savory appetizer to every get-together. Sometimes just for some variety, I'll roll one ball in chipped beef and the other ball in some chopped walnuts...it's delicious either way!

- 2 8-oz. pkgs. cream cheese, softened
- 4-oz. jar diced pimentos, drained
- 1/2 lb. dried, chipped beef, chopped and divided
- 1 bunch green onions, chopped
- 8-oz. pkg. finely shredded Cheddar cheese
- Worcestershire sauce to taste
- crackers and sliced veggies for dipping

1 In a bowl, mix together all ingredients except crackers and veggies, reserving 1/2 cup beef. Blend well. Form mixture into 2 equal balls.

2 Wrap balls in plastic wrap and refrigerate for at least one hour to overnight. Before serving, roll balls in reserved beef to coat. Serve with crackers and vegetables.

Serves 16 to 20

SWEET-AND-SOUR MEATBALLS

ANNETTE MEHL
BELL, FL

A quick & easy recipe my mom gave me several years ago. The ingredients may sound unusual, but these meatballs are always welcome at potlucks and get-togethers.

- 2 to 2-1/2 lbs. frozen meatballs, thawed
- 14-1/2 oz. can sauerkraut, drained
- 14-oz. can whole-berry cranberry sauce
- 12-oz. jar cocktail sauce
- 1 c. brown sugar, packed
- 1-1/2 c. water

1 Place meatballs in a lightly greased slow cooker. Add remaining ingredients; stir gently to coat. Cover and cook on low setting for 2 to 3 hours.

Serves 10 to 12

PUMPKIN PATCH CHEESE BALL

VICKIE
GOOSEBERRY PATCH

Makes a tasty cheese ball any time of year...but especially fun at Halloween!

16-oz. pkg. shredded extra-sharp Cheddar cheese
8-oz. pkg. cream cheese, softened
8-oz. container chive & onion cream cheese
2 t. paprika
1/2 t. cayenne pepper
honey-wheat twist pretzel
flat-leaf parsley leaves
assorted crackers

1 In a medium bowl, combine cheeses and spices. Cover and refrigerate for 4 hours.

2 Shape mixture into a ball; lightly press into a pumpkin shape. Smooth surface with a table knife. Press pretzel and parsley into top of cheese ball for pumpkin stem and leaf. Serve with crackers.

Makes 10 to 12 servings

SEASONED PRETZEL TWISTS

MICHELLE KUHN
GROVELAND, FL

My family loves to snack! Ordinary snack foods just don't have the same taste as homemade goodies, so I started making these pretzels for special movie nights at home. Semi-homemade and seasoned with a pinch of love. Enjoy!

32-oz. pkg. mini pretzel twists
1-oz. pkg. ranch salad dressing mix
1 T. dried dill weed
1/2 t. onion powder
1/2 t. garlic powder
1/2 t. celery salt
16-oz. bottle buttery popcorn oil

1 Place pretzels in a large bowl; set aside. In a separate bowl, mix together salad dressing mix and seasonings. Add popcorn oil; stir well. Drizzle oil mixture over pretzels; stir well to coat.

2 Let stand for 3 to 4 hours, stirring frequently, until pretzels are dry. May be served immediately.

Makes 8 to 10 servings

BAKED ARTICHOKE SQUARES

ELLEN FOLKMAN
CRYSTAL BEACH, FL

This is a recipe I remember my mom, Jennie Miller, making when I was young. It was popular with her friends and, being a great party hostess, she made it often. When she downsized last year, she handed me folders full of recipes she had collected over the years and I found this one among them. I made the squares recently for a potluck party and, just like years ago, they went very quickly!

- **2 6-oz. jars marinated artichoke hearts**
- **1/2 c. onion, chopped**
- **1 clove garlic, minced**
- **4 eggs, beaten**
- **1/4 c. dry bread crumbs**
- **1/2 t. fresh Italian parsley, chopped**
- **2 c. shredded Cheddar cheese**
- **salt and pepper to taste**

1 Drain liquid from one jar of artichokes into a skillet; drain liquid from remaining jar and discard. Chop all artichokes and set aside.

2 Heat liquid in skillet over medium heat. Sauté onion and garlic until soft; drain. In a bowl, combine eggs, bread crumbs and parsley. Stir in onion mixture, chopped artichokes, cheese, salt and pepper. Pour mixture into a greased 13"x9" baking pan. Bake at 325 degrees for 30 to 35 minutes. Cool; cut into small squares.

Serves 8 to 10

HOT & BUBBLY CHEESE DIP

LEE SMITH
PEMBROKE PINES, FL

Once you start eating it, it's impossible to stop...enjoy!

- **1 large round loaf bread**
- **2 8-oz. pkgs. cream cheese, softened**
- **8-oz. pkg. shredded Parmesan cheese**
- **8-oz. pkg. shredded mozzarella cheese**
- **16-oz. jar mayonnaise**
- **Optional: snack crackers, tortilla chips**

1 Hollow out loaf; cut pulled-out bread into small cubes and set aside. In a bowl, combine cheeses and mayonnaise. Spoon mixture into loaf; set on a baking sheet.

2 Bake at 350 degrees for 30 to 40 minutes, until bubbly and golden. Place loaf on a serving plate; surround with bread cubes. May also be served with crackers or chips.

Serves 12

JULIE'S FRESH GUACAMOLE

JULIE DOSSANTOS
FORT PIERCE, FL

I love guacamole! I like it to be creamy and a little chunky, all at the same time. This recipe is much more delicious than store-bought guacamole, and it's so simple to make.

6 avocados, halved and pitted
3 T. lime juice
1/2 yellow onion, finely chopped
4 roma tomatoes, chopped
3/4 c. sour cream
1 T. ranch salad dressing
1 T. salt, or to taste
1 T. pepper, or to taste
1 T. chili powder
1/2 t. cayenne pepper
Garnish: fresh cilantro sprigs
tortilla chips

1 Scoop out avocado pulp into a large bowl; mash with a fork. Add lime juice, onion and tomatoes; mix with a spoon. Add sour cream, salad dressing and seasonings; mix well.

2 Cover with plastic wrap; refrigerate for at least 30 minutes. Garnish with cilantro. Serve with tortilla chips.

Makes 8 to 10 servings

FLORIDA FUN

A true Caribbean delight is conch fritters, which are battered bites of fried conch.

SUNSHINE STATE SMOOTHIES

JULIE DOSSANTOS
FORT PIERCE, FL

This smoothie combines the citrus goodness from our home state of Florida with other healthful fruits and veggies.

1 Combine all ingredients except optional garnish in a blender. Process well for about one minute.

2 Pour into 2 glasses; garnish with fruit slices, if desired.

Serves 2

4 to 5 ice cubes
1 peach, halved, pitted and cubed
4-oz. container low-fat peach or vanilla yogurt
1 to 2 bananas, sliced
1/4 c. orange juice
10 baby carrots
Optional: orange or peach slices

SWEET SALSA

TRACI DOXTATOR
BRADENTON, FL

My friend Marcia and I had had such fun entertaining each other's families every weekend...and we built the most special friendship over salsa, chips and a deck of cards!

1 Stir together all ingredients except chips; cover and refrigerate for at least 30 minutes. Serve with tortilla chips.

Makes about 4-3/4 cups

2 c. cantaloupe, peeled, seeded and finely chopped
2 c. cherry tomatoes, chopped
1/4 c. green onions, chopped
1/4 c. fresh basil, chopped
2 T. jalapeño peppers, diced
2 T. lime juice
2 T. orange juice
1/4 t. salt
1/8 t. pepper
tortilla chips

UNCLE TOM'S FRESH TOMATO SALSA

DENISE JONES
FOUNTAIN, FL

My Uncle Tom Moore sent me this recipe when I was looking for tomato salsa recipes and it is the best one I've ever tried. Whenever I make a batch, it doesn't last long. I like to make lots of jars at once so I can give some away.

2 to 3 ripe tomatoes, chopped
1 clove garlic, minced
1 Anaheim green chile, cut into thirds and seeds removed
3 green onions, trimmed and cut into 1-inch pieces
4-oz. can chopped green chiles
1/4 c. fresh cilantro, chopped
1 T. lime juice
1 t. olive oil
salt and pepper to taste
Optional: 1 to 3 jalapeño peppers, seeds and veins removed, if desired
1/4 c. ice water

1 In a saucepan, combine all ingredients except ice water in the order listed. Bring to a boil over medium heat.

2 Remove from heat; stir in ice water and let stand a few minutes before serving. Keep refrigerated.

Makes 6 to 8 servings

TERRI'S HURRICANE DILL DIP

TERESA RAWNICK
PALM BAY, FL

In 1995, when we were in the eye of Hurricane Erin, my best friend & next-door neighbor Traci called to ask if there was take-out for my homemade dill dip. It was so quick & easy that I whipped up a batch and ran it next door before the winds picked up again. We've called it Terry's Hurricane Dill Dip ever since!

1 c. plain yogurt
1 c. mayonnaise
1 T. dill weed
1 T. dried, minced onion
1/2 t. seasoned salt
potato chips, assorted cut-up vegetables

1 Combine all ingredients except potato chips and vegetables; mix thoroughly.

2 Cover and chill for about one hour to blend flavors. Serve with your favorite chips or cut-up fresh vegetables.

Makes 2 cups

FUN FACT

Feeling tired in the afternoon? Put down the caffeinated soda and pick up a cucumber. Cucumbers are a good source of B vitamins and carbohydrates that can provide that quick pick-me-up that can last for hours.

BERRY-CITRUS SMOOTHIES

CHERI MAXWELL
GULF BREEZE, FL

A super-tasty, 3-ingredient recipe that's ready in a snap.

1 pt. strawberries, hulled and sliced
1 c. plain low-fat yogurt
1 c. frozen lemon or orange sorbet

1 Combine all ingredients in a blender; process until smooth. Pour into glasses to serve.

Makes 4 servings

CITRUS PUNCH

JANIS GREENE
BRANDON, FL

I make this any time of year. But when citrus is in season here, it is the best with slices of fresh fruit floating on top. A refreshing citrus punch your guests will love!

2 12-oz. cans frozen limeade concentrate, thawed
2 12-oz. can frozen lemonade concentrate, thawed
1-oz. bottle orange extract
6 c. water
3 ltrs. lemon-lime soda, chilled

1 Combine all ingredients in a large punch bowl; stir to mix well.

Serves 20

SPICY CITRUS CIDER

ELLEN FOLKMAN
CRYSTAL BEACH, FL

Keep this flavorful beverage warm in a slow cooker...everyone can help themselves.

8 c. apple juice
2-1/4 c. water
1-1/2 c. orange juice
1/4 c. molasses
3 4-inch cinnamon sticks
1 T. whole cloves
Garnish: apple and orange slices

1 Combine all ingredients except fruit slices in a large saucepan over medium heat.

2 Simmer for 10 minutes, stirring occasionally. Strain before serving. Garnish with fruit slices.

Makes about 3 quarts

SHRIMP DARCY

KRISTINA HILL
APOPKA, FL

This is a great appetizer to hold guests over until dinner is ready. Frozen shrimp may be used...just thaw and rinse well.

3 lbs. uncooked jumbo shrimp, peeled and cleaned
16-oz. bottle zesty Italian salad dressing
2 T. garlic, pressed
2 lemons, halved
1/4 c. fresh parsley, chopped
1 loaf garlic bread, sliced

1 In a 13"x9" glass baking pan, combine shrimp, salad dressing and garlic. Squeeze lemons over shrimp and add lemon halves to pan,cut-side up. Sprinkle parsley on top.

2 Bake, uncovered, at 350 degrees for 15 minutes. Stir; bake an additional 15 minutes. Serve shrimp with bread for dipping in pan juices.

Makes 6 to 10 servings

CHAPTER SIX

Time-for-a-Treat Desserts

YOU WOULDN'T THINK OF ENDING A MEAL WITHOUT JUST A LITTLE SOMETHING SWEET, SO ENJOY THESE DELICIOUS TREATS THAT PUT THE ICING ON THE CAKE.

BANANAS FOSTER FOR TWO

BETH KRAMER
PORT SAINT LUCIE, FL

After the kids have gone to bed, I stir up this luscious treat in a jiffy...it makes just enough for myself and a friend!

2 T. butter, sliced
1-1/2 T. brown sugar, packed
2 ripe bananas, sliced diagonally
1/2 t. rum extract
Garnish: vanilla ice cream

1 In a skillet over medium heat, bring butter, brown sugar and bananas just to a boil.

2 Cook and stir for 2 minutes. Add rum extract; cook and stir for 30 seconds. To serve, spoon over a scoop of ice cream.

Serves 2

FLORIDA FUN

Dade City is known as the kumquat capital of Florida. Eat kumquats out of hand, of course. Or they also show up in marmalade and desserts at various farmers' markets.

CHOCOLATE-HAZELNUT SKILLET BARS

CHERI MAXWELL
GULF BREEZE, FL

These blondie-like bars are too good to pass up. If you aren't a fan of hazelnuts, pecans, almonds or even peanuts would be just as tasty!

1-1/4 c. all-purpose flour
1/4 t. baking powder
1/2 t. baking soda
1/2 t. salt
1/2 c. butter
1 c. dark brown sugar, packed
1 egg, beaten
1-1/2 t. vanilla extract
1 t. espresso powder
3/4 c. dark baking chocolate, chopped
1/2 c. hazelnuts, chopped

1 In a bowl, combine flour, baking powder, baking soda and salt; set aside. Melt butter in a large cast-iron skillet over medium heat. Add brown sugar and whisk until sugar is dissolved, about one minute. Slowly pour butter mixture into flour mixture. Add egg, vanilla and espresso powder to flour mixture; stir until combined. Fold in remaining ingredients.

2 Spoon dough into skillet; bake at 350 degrees for 20 to 25 minutes, until golden on top and a toothpick tests clean. Let stand 30 minutes; slice into wedges to serve.

Serves 8

BLUEBERRY CREAM PIE

CAROL PATTERSON
DELTONA, FL

This delectable pie won me a blue ribbon at the county fair!

- **8-oz. container sour cream**
- **2 T. all-purpose flour**
- **3/4 c. sugar**
- **1 t. vanilla extract**
- **1/4 t. salt**
- **1 egg, beaten**
- **2-1/2 c. fresh blueberries**
- **9-inch pie crust, unbaked**

1 In a bowl, combine all ingredients except blueberries and crust. Beat with an electric mixer on high speed until well mixed, about 2 minutes. Fold in blueberries; pour into unbaked pie crust.

2 Bake at 400 degrees for 25 minutes; remove from oven. Sprinkle pie with topping; bake an additional 10 minutes. Chill before serving.

Serves 6 to 8

TOPPING

- **3 T. all-purpose flour**
- **1 T. sugar**
- **1-1/2 t. butter**
- **3 T. chopped pecans or walnuts**

1 Stir ingredients together until crumbly.

GRILLED PINEAPPLE SUNDAES

CHERI MAXWELL
GULF BREEZE, FL

Luscious! Grilling really transforms slices of juicy ripe pineapple.

1 In a bowl, mix brown sugar, butter, lemon juice and cinnamon. Brush mixture over both sides of pineapple slices. Grill pineapple over high heat for about one minute on each side, until golden.

2 Remove each slice to a dessert plate. Serve warm, topped with a scoop of ice cream and garnished as desired.

Serves 4 to 6

1/2 c. brown sugar, packed
2 T. butter, melted
2 T. lemon juice
1 t. cinnamon
1 pineapple, peeled, cored and sliced 1-inch thick
Garnish: vanilla ice cream
Optional: toasted coconut, maraschino cherries

KEY LIME CUPCAKES

JENNIE GIST
GOOSEBERRY PATCH

I spent the summer trying different-flavored cupcakes. I love lime, so this was my favorite!

1 In a large bowl, combine dry cake mix, soda and 1/4 cup key lime juice. Spray muffin cups with non-stick vegetable spray. Fill muffin cups 2/3 full.

2 Bake at 350 degrees for 12 minutes, or until a toothpick tests clean. Cool completely. Use a toothpick to poke several holes almost to the bottom of each cupcake; don't poke through bottoms. Mix together remaining lime juice, sweetened condensed milk and lime zest. Measure out 1/3 cup lime mixture; pour over all the cupcake tops. Stir whipped topping into the remaining lime mixture; chill for one hour. Frost cupcakes with whipped topping mixture. Garnish with coconut. Refrigerate until serving time.

Makes 2 dozen

16-oz. pkg. angel food cake mix
3/4 c. lemon-lime soda
1/2 c. plus 1 T. key lime juice, divided
14-oz. can sweetened condensed milk
1 t. lime zest
8-oz. container frozen whipped topping, thawed
Garnish: sweetened flaked coconut

CHERRY-ALMOND BUTTER BITES

SHARON JOHNSON
BOYNTON BEACH, FL

My favorite cookie of all time! I created this recipe by adapting my own ideas to recipes I had come across over the years. It is a sweet, tender cookie that's good year 'round.

3/4 c. slivered almonds
1 c. butter, softened
3/4 c. powdered sugar
1 t. vanilla extract
2-1/4 c. all-purpose flour
1/4 t. salt
8-oz. jar maraschino cherries, drained, 1 T. juice reserved and cherries cut in half
Garnish: red decorating sugar

1 In a food processor, finely grind almonds; set aside. In a bowl, mix butter, powdered sugar and vanilla until well blended. In a separate bowl, stir together flour, salt and almonds; blend flour mixture into butter mixture.

2 For each cookie, scoop a tablespoonful of dough; hollow out the center. Add a cherry half; pinch to seal. Place on parchment paper-lined baking sheets, one inch apart. Bake at 375 degrees until set and lightly golden, 8 to 9 minutes. Remove from oven; cool cookies on baking sheets until cool enough to handle. Dip tops of cookies in Cherry-Almond Icing; place on a wire rack set over wax paper to allow icing to cover the entire cookie top. Sprinkle with red sugar.

Makes about 3 dozen

CHERRY-ALMOND ICING

2 c. powdered sugar
1 T. reserved maraschino cherry juice
1 t. almond extract
2 to 3 T. milk

1 In a small bowl, stir together powdered sugar, cherry juice and extract. Thin with enough milk to make a dipping consistency.

JULIE'S STRAWBERRY YUM-YUM

JULIE HUTSON
CALLAHAN, FL

A wonderful, lighter strawberry trifle that's a snap to put together...this recipe is a winner!

- **2 3.3-oz. pkgs. instant sugar-free white chocolate pudding mix**
- **4 c. 1% milk**
- **1 baked angel food cake, torn into bite-size pieces and divided**
- **2 to 4 c. fresh strawberries, hulled sliced and divided**
- **2 8-oz. containers fat-free frozen whipped topping, thawed**
- **10-oz. pkg. coconut macaroon cookies, crushed and divided**

1 Beat dry pudding mix and milk with an electric mixer on low speed for 2 minutes. Chill for a few minutes,until thickened. In a large trifle bowl, layer half each of cake pieces, pudding and strawberries, one container whipped topping and half of crushed cookies.

2 Repeat layers, ending with cookies. Cover and chill until serving time.

Serves 8 to 10

COCONUT CRUNCH PRETZEL BARS

GLORIA SUCIU
PENSACOLA, FL

I make these scrumptious salty-sweet bars every year for special occasions. They're my daughter's favorite dessert! You won't be able to eat just one.

15-1/4 oz. pkg. German chocolate cake mix
1/2 c. pretzels, crushed
1/2 c. butter, melted
3 eggs, divided
1/4 c. sugar
1 c. dark corn syrup
1 c. pecans, chopped
1 c. butterscotch chips
2-1/4 c. sweetened flaked coconut
1 c. semi-sweet chocolate chips

1 In a large bowl, combine dry cake mix, pretzels, butter and one egg. Beat with an electric mixer on low speed until well blended. Press mixture into a 13"x9" baking pan that has been lined with aluminum foil and sprayed with non-stick vegetable spray.

2 Bake at 350 degrees for 15 minutes, or until crust puffs up and is dry. Cool 5 minutes. Meanwhile, combine sugar, corn syrup and remaining 2 eggs in a bowl. Beat with an electric mixer on low speed until well blended; fold in remaining ingredients. Spoon filling evenly over partially baked crust. Bake for 30 to 40 minutes longer, until edges are golden and center is almost set. Let cool one hour before slicing into bars.

Makes 3 dozen

CUSTARD RICE PUDDING

EDYTHE BOUQUIO
VERO BEACH, FL

I always make too much rice. My husband just loves rice pudding and this is a great way to use leftovers! I combined a few recipes to come up with this one, and he loves it. The custardy top is delish!

2 c. cooked rice
2-1/2 c. milk
3 eggs
1/2 c. sugar
1 t. vanilla extract
1/8 t. salt
Garnish: cinnamon or cinnamon-sugar to taste

1 Add cooked rice to a greased 2-quart casserole dish; set aside. In a small saucepan over low heat, bring milk just to boiling; remove from heat. Combine eggs, sugar, vanilla and salt in a blender. With blender running on low, slowly add warm milk and blend to combine. Pour over rice; sprinkle with cinnamon or cinnamon-sugar. Set dish in a large roasting pan.

2 Carefully pour hot water into roasting pan around dish, filling halfway up the sides of dish. Bake, uncovered, at 350 degrees for one hour, or until a knife tip inserted in center comes out clean. Remove roasting pan carefully from oven; let casserole dish stand in hot-water bath until dish is easy to handle. Serve warm or chilled.

Makes 6 servings

LEMON CRUNCH POUND CAKE

SHARON JONES
FOUNTAIN, FL

This is the best lemon pound cake I've ever made...everyone loves it! I enjoy serving it to special morning coffee guests...my mom, a neighbor or a group of ladies from church. I hope you love it too!

18-1/4 oz. pkg. yellow cake mix
3-oz. pkg. lemon gelatin mix
2/3 c. oil
4 eggs, beaten
3/4 c. water
1 t. lemon extract
1/2 t. salt
1/2 c. chopped pecans

1 In a large bowl, combine dry cake and gelatin mixes. Add remaining ingredients except pecans; beat well until smooth. Spray a Bundt® pan with non-stick vegetable spray; sprinkle with flour and shake out loose flour. Sprinkle pecans in bottom of pan; pour in batter.

2 Bake at 325 degrees for 45 to 55 minutes, until a toothpick tests clean. Cool cake completely; turn out of pan onto a serving plate. Drizzle with Powdered Sugar Glaze shortly before serving.

Makes about 12 servings

POWDERED SUGAR GLAZE

2 c. powdered sugar
3 T. milk
1/2 t. vanilla extract

1 Mix together powdered sugar and milk to desired thickness for drizzling; stir in vanilla.

OVER-THE-TOP PIE

EVELYN YEARTY
GULF HAMMOCK, FL

This makes three frozen pies...terrific for potlucks, parties and impromptu desserts! So easy to make and serve. Everyone who tastes a piece, wants the recipe!

1/2 c. butter
1/2 c. flaked coconut
1-1/2 c. chopped pecans
8-oz. pkg. cream cheese, softened
14-oz. can sweetened condensed milk
16-oz. container frozen whipped topping, thawed
3 9-inch shortbread crumb crusts
11-1/2 oz. jar salted caramel topping

1 Melt butter in a skillet over medium heat. Add coconut and pecans; cook and stir until toasted, about 5 to 7 minutes. Remove from heat; cool completely. In a bowl, combine cream cheese, condensed milk and whipped topping; stir until well blended. Divide mixture among the crusts.

2 Sprinkle coconut mixture evenly over pies; drizzle with caramel topping. Cover and freeze overnight; thaw slightly before slicing.

Makes 3 pies, 8 servings each

MOM'S PUMPKIN BROWNIES

LINDA RENDERER
OCALA, FL

Mom always made these terrific brownies on Halloween before we went out trick-or-treating.

4 eggs, room temperature
2 c. sugar
1 c. butter, melted and slightly cooled
1 c. canned pumpkin
1 t. vanilla extract
1-1/2 c. all-purpose flour
1-1/2 t. pumpkin pie spice
1/2 t. cinnamon
Garnish: vanilla or cream cheese frosting

1 In a large bowl, beat eggs well with an electric mixer on medium speed. Beat in sugar, butter, pumpkin and vanilla on medium speed. Add flour and spices; beat on low speed. Spread batter in a lightly greased 9"x9" baking pan.

2 Bake at 350 degrees for 40 minutes. Cool; frost as desired and cut into squares.

Makes 8 to 10

CRUSTLESS COCONUT PIE

GLENDA GEOHAGEN
DEFUNIAK SPRINGS, FL

This recipe makes 2 yummy pies...one to keep and on to give away!

4 eggs
1 c. sugar
2 c. skim milk
3 T. butter, melted
1/2 c. self-rising flour
1 t. vanilla extract
1/2 c. unsweetened flaked coconut, divided
Garnish: lime slices

1 Beat eggs at medium speed with an electric mixer until frothy. Add sugar and next 4 ingredients; beat well. Place 1/4 cup unsweetened coconut in each of 2 shallow, lightly greased 9" pie plates; pour half of filling mixture into each pie plate, stirring gently to distribute coconut.

2 Bake at 350 degrees for 25 to 30 minutes or until golden. Garnish with lime slices.

Makes 2 pies, each makes 6 servings

MINI CHEESECAKES

MICHELE ELLIS
PALM HARBOR, FL

Here is one of my favorite cheesecake recipes, given to me by one of my sisters. I like it because it is so fast, so easy and so good. Top with fresh fruit, canned pie filling, chocolate sauce or preserves...be creative!

12 vanilla wafers
2 8-oz. pkgs. cream cheese, softened
1/2 c. sugar
1 t. vanilla extract
2 eggs

1 Line a muffin tin with aluminum foil muffin cups. Place a vanilla wafer in each cup. In a bowl, beat together cream cheese, sugar and vanilla with an electric mixer on medium speed until fluffy. Add eggs, one at a time, beating after each addition, until well blended. Spoon cream cheese mixture over wafers, filling cups 3/4 full.

2 Bake at 325 degrees for 25 minutes; let cool.

Makes 12 mini cheesecakes

FLORIDA FUN

In the 1980s a bunch of tourists were frustrated, because they couldn't find good candy treats to take home to friends as souvenirs of Florida. So a company called Anastasia Confections came to the rescue. It perfected Coconut Patties, which became a hit as a special Florida treat. They have a shredded coconut center and are dipped in dark chocolate.

PEANUT BUTTER COOKIES IN A WINK

LYNNETTE ROHDE
HOLIDAY, FL

This is a very simple recipe my son and I would make together after a busy "little school dude and single working mom" crazy day...warm, fast and fresh flourless cookies!

- **1 c. creamy peanut butter**
- **1 c. sugar**
- **1 egg, beaten**
- **1 t. baking soda**

1 Mix together all ingredients until well blended. Roll dough into one-inch balls; place on ungreased baking sheets. Bake at 325 degrees for 8 to 10 minutes. Remove from oven; cool on baking sheets until set, about 5 minutes. Remove cookies to wire racks to finish cooling.

Makes 3 dozen

VALARIE'S DESSERT BURRITOS

VALARIE DENNARD
PALATKA, FL

This is a tropical alternative to s'mores. Enjoy them at the beach, over a campfire or even while tailgating!

- **4 10-inch flour tortillas**
- **2 c. mini marshmallows**
- **8-oz. can crushed pineapple, drained**
- **1/4 c. sweetened flaked coconut**

1 Arrange tortillas on separate sheets of aluminum foil. Divide marshmallows, pineapple and coconut down the center of each tortilla. Fold bottom third of tortilla over filling; fold one side in toward center and then fold the top over.

2 Fold and seal edges of foil around tortilla and bake on a campfire grate over medium coals for 7 to 10 minutes.

Makes 4 servings

TAHITIAN RICE PUDDING

BETH KRAMER
PORT SAINT LUCIE, FL

You will love this creamy dessert that is so easy to make!

3/4 c. long-cooking rice, uncooked
15-oz. can cream of coconut
12-oz. can evaporated milk
2-3/4 c. water
Optional: 1 T. dark rum
2/3 c. sweetened flaked coconut

1 Stir together rice, cream, milk and water in a 3 to 4-quart slow cooker until combined. Cover and cook on low setting for 4 to 5 hours. Remove crock from slow cooker. Stir in rum, if desired.

2 Let pudding cool for 10 minutes. Heat a small non-stick skillet over medium heat. Add coconut; cook and stir for 4 to 5 minutes, until toasted. Remove coconut and set aside. Spoon pudding into dessert bowls; sprinkle with toasted coconut.

Serves 6 to 8

SOUR CREAM SCONES

ELAINE ANDERSON
ALIQUIPPA, FL

Bake up some tender scones with ingredients you probably already have on hand. Serve with butter and jam...yum!

2 c. all-purpose flour
2 t. baking powder
1/2 t. baking soda
1/2 t. salt
1/4 c. butter
2 eggs, beaten
1/2 c. sour cream

1 Combine flour, baking powder, baking soda and salt; cut in butter until mixture resembles coarse crumbs. In a separate bowl, mix eggs and sour cream; stir into flour mixture until dough leaves the sides of the bowl. Knead for one minute.

2 On a floured surface, roll out dough into a 9-inch by 6-inch rectangle. Cut into 6, 3-inch by 3-inch squares; cut each square diagonally. Arrange scones on an ungreased baking sheet, 2 inches apart. Bake at 400 degrees for 10 to 12 minutes.

Makes one dozen

WHITE CHOCOLATE-CHERRY SCONES

CHERI MAXWELL
GULF BREEZE, FL

My best girlfriends and I always get together for a simple brunch in December, then go Christmas shopping. We especially like these yummy scones!

- **3 c. all-purpose flour**
- **1/2 c. sugar**
- **2-1/2 t. baking powder**
- **1/2 t. baking soda**
- **6 T. butter, softened**
- **1 c. vanilla yogurt**
- **6 T. milk, divided**
- **1-1/3 c. sweetened dried cherries**
- **2/3 c. white chocolate chips**

1 In a large bowl, combine flour, sugar, baking powder and baking soda. Cut in butter with a fork until mixture resembles coarse crumbs; set aside. In a small bowl, combine yogurt and 4 tablespoons milk. Stir into crumb mixture just until moistened. Mix in cherries and chocolate chips.

2 Pat dough into a 9-inch circle on an ungreased baking sheet. Cut into 8 wedges; gently separate wedges. Brush with remaining milk. Bake at 400 degrees for 20 to 25 minutes, until golden.

Makes 8 scones

SCHOOL LUNCH PEANUT BUTTER BARS

SHARON JONES
FOUNTAIN, FL

Remember the great-tasting peanut butter bars in the school lunchroom? This is it! I searched & searched, finally getting this recipe from a school lunchroom manager a few years ago. Yummy!

- **16-oz. pkg. graham crackers, crushed**
- **2 T. butter, room temperature**
- **1-1/2 to 2 16-oz. jars creamy peanut butter**
- **16-oz. pkg. powdered sugar, divided**

1 In a bowl, gradually mix cracker crumbs, butter and enough peanut butter to make a stiff mixture. Set aside 1/4 cup powdered sugar. Add remaining powdered sugar, a little at a time, to peanut butter mixture, using your hands. to mix. Press mixture 1/2-inch thick onto a wax paper-lined baking sheet. Sprinkle with reserved powdered sugar. Cover and refrigerate for about one hour. Cut into one-inch squares. Cover tightly and refrigerate for several days, or wrap and freeze for up to 2 months.

Makes 2 dozen

SWEDISH HORNS

LIZ CESAL
TAMPA, FL

I make these crescent-shaped cookies every Christmas and our family really loves them. The recipe was handed down from my grandmother to my mother, then to me.

- **1 lb. butter, room temperature**
- **4 c. all-purpose flour**
- **4 egg yolks, beaten, room temperature**
- **16-oz. container sour cream, room temperature**
- **1/2 to 1 c. powdered sugar**
- **12-oz. jar peach or apricot preserves**
- **Garnish: additional powdered sugar**

1 In a large bowl, blend butter with flour, using your hands. Mix in egg yolks and sour cream; dough will be sticky. Form dough into 15 balls, each 2 inches in diameter. Place balls in a bowl; cover and refrigerate overnight.

2 Lightly sprinkle powdered sugar over the work surface. Roll out balls, one at a time, into 6-inch circles; cut each circle into 5 triangles. Spoon 1/2 teaspoon preserves onto each triangle. Roll up, starting at the wide end; tuck in ends and curve into a half-moon shape. Place cookies on greased baking sheets.

3 Bake at 350 degrees for 30 to 35 minutes. Cool; sprinkle with powdered sugar.

Makes about 6 dozen

COCONUT MACAROONS

VICKIE
GOOSEBERRY PATCH

An old-fashioned treat...we just love these sweet, chewy little morsels of coconut.

4 egg whites, beaten
1 t. vanilla extract
1/8 t. almond extract
3/4 c. sugar
1/4 t. salt
3 c. sweetened flaked coconut

1 In a large bowl, whisk together all ingredients except coconut. Add coconut; mix well. Drop by rounded teaspoonfuls onto parchment paper-lined baking sheets.

2 Bake at 325 degrees for about 25 minutes, or until set and golden; rotate baking sheets between upper and lower oven racks halfway through baking time. Cool on baking sheets for one minute; transfer to wire racks and cool completely. Store in an airtight container.

Makes about 3-1/2 dozen

FLORIDA FUN

You don't have to go to the southern tip of the state for one of Florida's treasured delicacies. Key Lime Pie is good anywhere you are lucky to have some.

SIMPLE SUGAR COOKIES

JULIE DOSSANTOS
FORT PIERCE, FL

These drop cookies are perfect for holidays year 'round. They're a bit crisp on the outside and soft and chewy on the inside. Use colored sugar sprinkles for the season...orange and purple for Halloween, pink and red for Valentine's Day. Have a little fun with these!

1/2 c. butter, softened
1 c. sugar
1 egg, beaten
1 T. half-and-half or milk
1 t. vanilla extract
1-1/2 c. all-purpose flour
1 t. baking powder
1/4 t. salt
Garnish: 1/2 to 3/4 c. colored sprinkles or sugar

1 In a bowl, beat together butter, sugar, egg, half-and-half or milk and vanilla. In separate bowl, mix together flour, baking powder and salt. Add to butter mixture; stir thoroughly.

2 Cover and refrigerate for 20 minutes. Drop dough by teaspoonfuls onto parchment paper-covered baking sheets, one inch apart. Top with sprinkles or sugar.

3 Bake at 375 degrees for 8 to 9 minutes, until lightly golden around edges. Let cookies cool on baking sheet for one minute; transfer to a wire rack and cool completely.

Makes 4 dozen

INDEX

Appetizers/Snacks

Beverages

Breakfast/Breads

Desserts

Mains

Beef

Fish

Pork

Poultry

Vegetarian

Salads

Sandwiches

Sides

Soups

U.S. to METRIC RECIPE EQUIVALENTS

Volume Measurements

¼ teaspoon	1 mL
½ teaspoon	2 mL
1 teaspoon	5 mL
1 tablespoon = 3 teaspoons	15 mL
2 tablespoons = 1 fluid ounce	30 mL
¼ cup	60 mL
⅓ cup	75 mL
½ cup = 4 fluid ounces	125 mL
1 cup = 8 fluid ounces	250 mL
2 cups = 1 pint = 16 fluid ounces	500 mL
4 cups = 1 quart	1 L

Weights

1 ounce	30 g
4 ounces	120 g
8 ounces	225 g
16 ounces = 1 pound	450 g

Baking Pan Sizes

Square

8x8x2 inches	2 L = 20x20x5 cm
9x9x2 inches	2.5 L = 23x23x5 cm

Rectangular

13x9x2 inches	3.5 L = 33x23x5 cm

Loaf

9x5x3 inches	2 L = 23x13x7 cm

Round

8x1½ inches	1.2 L = 20x4 cm
9x1½ inches	1.5 L = 23x4 cm

Recipe Abbreviations

t. = teaspoon	ltr. = liter
T. = tablespoon	oz. = ounce
c. = cup	lb. = pound
pt. = pint	doz. = dozen
qt. = quart	pkg. = package
gal. = gallon	env. = envelope

Oven Temperatures

300° F	150° C
325° F	160° C
350° F	180° C
375° F	190° C
400° F	200° C
450° F	230° C

Kitchen Measurements

A pinch = ⅛ tablespoon
1 fluid ounce = 2 tablespoons
3 teaspoons = 1 tablespoon
4 fluid ounces = ½ cup
2 tablespoons = ⅛ cup
8 fluid ounces = 1 cup
4 tablespoons = ¼ cup
16 fluid ounces = 1 pint
8 tablespoons = ½ cup
32 fluid ounces = 1 quart
16 tablespoons = 1 cup
16 ounces net weight = 1 pound
2 cups = 1 pint
4 cups = 1 quart
4 quarts = 1 gallon

Send us your favorite recipe

and the memory that makes it special for you!*

If we select your recipe for a brand-new **Gooseberry Patch** cookbook, your name will appear right along with it...and you'll receive a FREE copy of the book!

Submit your recipe on our website at

www.gooseberrypatch.com/sharearecipe

*Please include the number of servings and all other necessary information.

Have a taste for more?

Visit www.gooseberrypatch.com to join our Circle of Friends!

- Free recipes, tips and ideas plus a complete cookbook index
- Get mouthwatering recipes and special email offers delivered to your inbox.

You'll also love these cookbooks from **Gooseberry Patch**!

5-Ingredient Family Favorite Recipes
America's Comfort Foods
Best Church Suppers
Best-Ever Cookie, Brownie & Bar Recipes
Best-Ever Sheet Pan & Skillet Recipes
Cozy Christmas Comforts
Delicious Recipes for Diabetics
Harvest Homestyle Meals
Healthy, Happy, Homemade Meals
Meals in Minutes: 15, 20, 30

www.gooseberrypatch.com